GOOD DISCIPLINE, GOOD KIDS

Gerald E. Nelson, M.D.

Adams Media Corporation
Holbrook, Massachusetts

I dedicate this book to my children, Peter and Isabelle, Sara, Annika and Denis, and my grandson, Sam.

Copyright ©2000, Gerald E. Nelson. All rights reserved.
This book, or parts thereof, may not be reproduced in any form
without permission from the publisher; exceptions are made for brief
excerpts used in published reviews.

Published by
Adams Media Corporation
260 Center Street, Holbrook, MA 02343. U.S.A.
www.adamsmedia.com

ISBN: 1-58062-284-4

Printed in Canada.

J I H G F E D C B

Library of Congress Cataloging-in-Publication data
available upon request from the publisher.

This publication is designed to provide accurate and authoritative information with regard to the subject matter covered. It is sold with the understanding that the publisher is not engaged in rendering legal, accounting, or other professional advice. If legal advice or other expert assistance is required, the services of a competent professional person should be sought.

　　　　— From a *Declaration of Principles* jointly adopted by a Committee of the American Bar Association and a Committee of Publishers and Associations

Cover photo ©Bill Tucker/International Stock

This book is available at quantity discounts for bulk purchases.
For information, call 1-800-872-5627.

Table of Contents

Acknowledgments

Every book owes its existence to many persons. I am especially grateful to Dennis Clark for his patient assistance and clear thinking and prodding me to "stay on task." I am grateful to Richard Lewak for his knowledgeable insights and wisdom and for helping me conceive and implement the "one-minute" concept. Bryan Court helped write, edit, and reorganize the book for this edition. His clear thinking, combined with his organizational skills and careful attention to detail, made this revision a pleasant experience. He has increased the value of the book immeasurably. Lastly, I want to thank Gertrud Mueller Nelson for her love, patience, and able assistance in writing the manuscript.

For the privacy of my patients, the examples I use in this book are composites or inventions with names and details changed and shuffled to make them unidentifiable. But it is to the children and parents in my practice that I am especially grateful. It is their acceptance and careful implementation of the One-Minute Scolding and the different attachment techniques that gave flesh to the concept and thrilling hope for a solution to others.

Introduction

Good discipline is at the heart of the teaching process by which children learn how to function as happy and effective members of society. As such, discipline is one of the most important elements of family life, yet it is also one of the most troublesome and least understood.

Our intent is not to fill the scholarly vacuum by addressing a technical study to our professional colleagues. On the contrary, we want to speak in plain language to all those frustrated parents, grandparents, teachers, and others who have accepted the responsibility of nurturing children. We have developed an approach to discipline that is easy and really works. We call it the One-Minute Scolding.

So before you put this book down, take a look at Chapter 8. If you recognize yourself or your children there, you have a problem. You also have a solution: the One-Minute Scolding. Chapter 8 gives a detailed, how-to description of the approach.

Chapter 1

About This Book

Good Discipline, Good Kids is a book about discipline—discipline that works. Its format is simple, and its disciplining method leaves both parent and child feeling good about themselves and each other. This unique form of discipline tells the child clearly what rule has been broken and how the parent feels about the rule being broken. Yet it also tells the child that he or she is loved and cared for by the parent. Finally, it does what good discipline is supposed to do: it puts a stop to a child's unwanted behavior, but even more, it teaches him or her appropriate behavior. We call this disciplinary strategy the One-Minute Scolding.

Why Children Want Discipline

Children like knowing how to behave. Correct behavior increases their sense of autonomy and security. Their good behavior and confidence also happens to please those around them. They are not against being agreeable and affording enjoyment to others, and that feels good to them.

But appropriate behavior and reasonable choices don't always bloom naturally in children. Good behaviors are not "built in." They are learned. Discipline is one of the most important ways that parents teach behavior and impart values to their children. True discipline is a teaching tool, not a punishment.

Successful and happy discipline follows the child out of his home and into his wider world. As he grows, he is more and more secure in knowing how to act at school, on the playing field, or at his friend's house. His friends and his teachers appreciate his ability to express himself honestly and to handle disappointments, control his anger, and share his joys. He is welcomed because he wants to "play by the rules." His teacher is pleased and effective as she works with him because he knows how to listen, contribute, work, learn, and interact in the classroom.

Although some of those in society have learned good behavior, many have not. Our society is torn and troubled by those people who have never learned how to behave by the rules or contribute positively. The rising rate of juvenile delinquency and crime exposes the difficulty parents face in teaching their children values and appropriate behaviors.

Parents Need Support

Does it help to blame parents when children don't behave well? Most parents love their children and want to do their best in guiding and teaching them. Even at their best, parents have bouts with uncertainty and defeat. When stressed, any parent is tempted to revert to past experience and reuse a disciplinary action from his or her own childhood. This is true even when parents acknowledge that the overall effect of their own childhood discipline was negative. Most parents realize that these "old-fashioned" disciplines won't work. They remember their feelings of sadness and anger if they were shamed and threatened into submission when they were children. Many parents know firsthand how fears and hurts have followed them into their adulthood as a result of caustic put-downs, slaps, restrictions, or beatings. They remember far better the punishments than the "crimes." Parents don't want to repeat that for their own children.

One may argue that the old punishments did work at one time. After all, they successfully suppressed unwanted behavior. But the price was too high. And what did they teach? Many adults feel the results of those experiences manifested in fears, neurotic guilt, low self-esteem, lack of trust, and inability to risk. Today, parents want an effective discipline that teaches good behavior, but even more, one that results in good warm relationships with their children. They want a discipline that allows the child to grow into a warm, trusting adult who relates well to others.

Because parents have given up on the "old-fashioned" ways, however, does not mean that they believe in the permissive approach that a few "authorities" espoused in the recent past. They do not want their children to "run wild" with vigorous, unharnessed energy and boundless freedom to tyrannize their family and neighborhood with obnoxious, self-indulgent, controlling behaviors that know no limits. Parents today know that discipline is absolutely necessary, but they are not at all certain what constitutes this "good discipline."

A New Approach

In our practice over the past twenty-five years, we have worked with troubled children and their families. Some of these children were especially troubled and difficult because they had suffered multiple losses of parents and foster families. The more losses these children suffered, the more difficult they were to discipline. And the more difficult they were, the more they were passed from foster family to foster family, or from therapist to therapist. Everyone wanted to give up on them eventually, even though parents and therapists had taken them on initially with hope and love and positive feelings. We saw these children creating an endless and increasingly painful cycle of behaviors caused by loss and resulting in more loss. It was a tragically painful cycle that love and the best of intentions alone could not break for these children. The usual punishments and disciplines made little or no impact. Their inappropriate and even dangerous behaviors escalated to a point where their worst fear— abandonment—came true.

Everything we heard and saw pointed to the need for a whole new form of discipline. We felt that a new solution was called for especially in the cases of these children who were caught in the cycle of repeated poor behavior and repeated loss. Something had to break this cycle and repair the wounds. What kind of discipline could these children respond to?

The One-Minute Scolding arose out of that need. It was a strategy that worked so well for these very troubled children and their foster or adoptive parents that we began teaching it to parents who were single or divorced and whose children were struggling with loss. We taught it to teachers and mental health workers. We also began teaching it to parents of less troubled children and to parents of children who had no particular psychopathology. Its effectiveness was astonishing on a number of levels:

* The One-Minute Scolding changed the poor behavior of all kinds of children.
* The technique taught parents to be effective teachers of proper behaviors and values.
* It strengthened the bond between mildly troubled children and their parents.
* It created a bond between children and their foster or adoptive parents by repairing the child's ability to form attachments.
* It left both parents and children feeling good about themselves and each other; they became stronger, happier people.

This is what discipline should produce and, with the aid of this book, what you will achieve. The actual directions for the One-Minute Scolding (addressed in Part II) are simple, but the implementation takes practice. Read this book carefully and use it as a "hands-on" tool until you have mastered the technique.

This book will guide you through the principles of the One-Minute Scolding:

* It explains the development of the underlying theory.
* It shows how the One-Minute Scolding works as good discipline and not punishment.
* It discusses when to use it and guides you through the common difficulties.

* It describes how to adapt the One-Minute Scolding to children of various ages and temperaments.
* It explains how the Scolding helps children develop a conscience.

The effectiveness of the One-Minute Scolding is enhanced by the fact that it can be used by all parents for children in all situations when children need discipline. It is not only a technique but also an attitude and a philosophy, briefly applied. It is not the only discipline that a parent should use, because children need to be taught in many ways. It cannot make parenting easy, but it can make discipline easy, reasonable, fair, and consistent for both parent and child. The technique we describe can be used by step-father as well as natural father, mother, stepmother, and even uncle and aunt. This provides welcome continuity and consistency for the child. Whatever your parenting situation, the technique we use to discipline children is effective and fair. It not only teaches rules and behavior, it teaches values and how to express feelings. It is designed to promote parent-child dialogue and attachment. It compels the parent to be clear about rules, and yet children have a chance to influence rule making. It is thoughtful, but it takes only a minute.

The Elements
of Discipline—
What Works,
What Doesn't

Chapter 2

Who's in Charge?

"Who's the boss?" The very question makes most people cringe. The idea of parents being "bosses" seems dated and authoritarian. These days people stress cooperation and consensus as keys to successful relationships. The word boss conjures up an image of unfairness, harsh discipline, and unreasonableness, and it might awaken thoughts of children being "seen and not heard." Many parents remember being treated with harsh, unreasonable punishment. They remember when children standing up for themselves were said to be "smart-mouthing" or "back-talking." Nobody wants those days back. However, many parents, frightened of repeating their own parents' mistakes, have given up being parents who are in charge of and responsible for their children. They don't want to discipline their children the way they were taught, but they do not know what to do instead. Afraid to make mistakes, they take no stand at all on their children's behavior and values. They hope that their children will eventually learn on their own.

Children do eventually learn from this hands-off approach, but not what their parents want them to learn. Often they learn that they cannot count on their parents to prepare them for future experiences, so they depend on themselves. They frequently fail, so they anticipate failure and develop an apathetic attitude. They assume that all adults have the same attitude as their parents, so they manipulate and control their teachers and other adults in authority. Since they are "in control" or the "boss" at home, they assume that is their role in school, in restaurants, and elsewhere in the community. Children who are in control at home are miserable at home and at school, and they make everyone else equally unhappy. Parents must be the boss, for the welfare of their children. They are responsible to the rest of the community to teach their children how to behave, how to relate, and what values to hold.

The goal of parenting is twofold. On the more basic level, parents protect and nurture children so that they can grow and thrive. Beyond this, parents endeavor to teach children how to live full, productive, and happy lives. Parenting is a huge undertaking, and the commitment is often for life. To undertake a lifelong commitment without fully understanding your goals and methods is unwise. You can't succeed if you hate making decisions or taking responsibility for others, because you are going to do both as a parent. If you are going to be an effective parent and teach your child how to live life productively and happily, then you also have to have some self-awareness, some sense of what works for you and what doesn't. Yet knowing what values work for you is not enough; you still have to teach them to your child. The technique we describe in this book is one that helps parents teach these values and ways of behaving to their children. At the same time, our technique fulfills the basic goal of parenting, helping a child feel safe, nurtured, and protected.

Being the Right Kind of Boss for Your Child

Why is being in control, being the boss, so important? Children are born with a basic personality but without knowledge. Experience, and especially the experience of being parented, may enhance those traits in children that are beneficial. Good experiences can make difficult personality traits manageable. Bad experiences can make managing difficult traits impossible. For example, some children are genetically inclined to have high energy. They are restless, hard to settle down. They struggle and squirm and, as they grow, they resist discipline. They want things their own way. They demand more of everything and want it sooner than children with a more even energy level. These high-energy children get bored quickly and are drawn to excitement. Parents often notice these traits early in their child's life. This particular trait of having high energy is not bad or good—it is just one way a child is "wired." Having a high-energy child may be positive. However, parents have to know how to provide children with the best environment for them to learn to use their energy wisely. It is important that a child learn to like himself and his personality. A high-energy child who was not well-parented could become an angry, rebellious child, always struggling with authority. On the other hand, the same child who was well-parented could become a highly productive, cheerful leader as an adult.

Another example of an inborn trait is general sensitivity. As infants, highly sensitive children respond immediately and loudly to small changes in their environment. They cry, for example, if the milk is not quite right, and they scream if they are uncomfortable. As they grow, they tend to cry easily when they are frustrated or slightly upset. Often, they are called babies or immature, but really they are just more sensitive than other children and respond with more pain to events that don't seem to affect others. When a parent gets a little angry, the sensitive child may feel devastated. Punishment is often overwhelming to them. Small losses or setbacks can be experienced as traumatic by these sensitive children. On the other end of the scale are children who are not very sensitive. They need a more vigorous stimulus before they respond. Saying "no" quietly but firmly might be taken by the highly sensitive child as a rejection rather than guidance or parenting, and by the less sensitive child as "not really no." While this book does not categorically address different personality traits, it does describe a technique that can be used with all children regardless of their basic personality structure.

Knowing your child's basic, inherited personality is important if you are to be a good boss. It is important to get to know children by observing them and looking at the way they consistently respond to their world. If you are unsure about the nature of your child's personality, discuss it with your spouse, friends, and relatives. Sometimes you need others to help you see your child clearly. Remember, children are not born with knowledge; they are born with a temperament and some basic human responses. The job of parenting is to know your child's temperament and set guidelines according to that temperament. Applying this to our examples, high-energy children tend to push themselves until they are exhausted. Sensitive children, on the other hand, may not push themselves without encouragement. It is important for parents to set limits for children who think they have unlimited ability and to encourage children who don't believe they have any ability at all.

Kids Need Parents to Be in Charge

Parents can help children to know themselves. For example, a parent can help a high-energy child avoid overreaching by telling her, "Amanda, there you go again, biting off more than you can chew—let's help you be a little more realistic." On the other hand, a sensitive child may be instilled with confidence by hearing, "Johnny, you know how you get frightened that you are not going to be good enough—why don't you try anyway; it usually works out for you."

Children need parents to be in charge. Remember that children are easily frightened. The world is a scary place for them, especially if they feel no one is in charge. Imagine that you, as an adult, have never left your neighborhood and are suddenly sent off to China or Russia on your own. What would it be like if you had no idea how to behave or didn't know what was allowed and what wasn't? Imagine that you couldn't communicate with people and didn't know what questions to ask in the first place. In this kind of situation, you would probably feel terribly insecure and afraid. You would feel unable to take any kind of risk because you wouldn't know what the consequences might be. You might become immobilized, or impulsively take chances and make mistakes. If someone took charge of you and kindly explained how to behave and what to expect from your strange and exotic surroundings, you would relax and enjoy your visit. In the same way, children need someone to guide them. They need someone to tell them about the dangers. If children know the consequences that follow from their behavior, they feel protected and secure. It is important then for parents and caretakers to be in charge so that children feel safe.

Parents need to be in control because children are sensitive creatures who have not yet built up a protective coat of understanding to help them handle an often cruel world. Children are prepared to learn. They are curious and constantly motivated to explore their environment. However, small children are also vulnerable and fearful because of their inability to protect and care for themselves. If children are in a situation where they feel uncared for and unprotected (when a parent or caretaker is gone for a long period of time, or when children are being cared for by a hostile or indifferent person), then these children will eventually "numb out" their stressful feeling of fear. This is to protect themselves. Think about a situation in which you were under a lot of stress for a long time. Maybe a divorce or difficult financial problem comes to mind. After much effort and pain, perhaps, you became "tired of caring." For children, the problem with this reaction to stress is that if they stop feeling, then they can't feel how others feel. They lose their capacity for empathy. When children lose their ability to be sensitive to the feelings of others, they become handicapped in their ability to develop a conscience. Conscience develops when children anticipate how bad they will feel if they should do something that would make a parent feel angry or hurt. If children don't care about consequences, they don't develop a conscience. Parents, therefore, need to be in charge—observing their children to see if they are under too much stress, to make sure the children don't respond to their world by numbing out their feelings.

Why Have Parents Lost Control of Their Children?

Many parents are having difficulty parenting their children. Crime and pregnancies among teenagers are on the upswing. Juvenile delinquency, teenage depression and suicide, as well as widespread drug and alcohol abuse, are serious problems. Clearly, many children are not learning how to behave and how to relate to each other and their parents. Their values are not those of the larger community. How has this happened? We think the answer is that parenting today is no longer as simple as it once was.

Parents were usually two people, a mother and a father, raising their children in a stable community surrounded and supported by family and friends who had similar values and expectations of children. The situation has changed radically in the last thirty years. We believe the rising divorce rate, leaving many children with single parents, and the rapid increase in two-career families have created a need for a revolution in child rearing. The old notion that children need to be protected and safeguarded against the brutal side of the adult world seems to have disappeared. Parents preoccupied with their own lives have tended to let the television act as a sedative or a pacifier for children. At the same time, parents have been unable to protect their children from all aspects of the adult world. Many parents don't have the energy after a full day's work to shelter their child, so they have come to believe the child can handle the realities of an adult world. In fact, many parents feel that children ought to be told the whole truth in order to prepare them for the exigencies of the adult world. It is not unusual for us to hear that parents tell their very young children, "Mommy and Daddy no longer live with each other because we no longer love each other. Daddy has a girlfriend and doesn't want to be with Mommy anymore."

New Challenges of Family Life

Family life has significantly changed. Rarely is there an extended family nearby—grandparents, cousins, uncles, and aunts. There is no supportive, stable community with similar values and expectations. Even more important, fewer children are being raised by both mother and father. We have single mothers and single fathers, adoptive single parents, single working mothers, adoptive gay and lesbian parents, stepparents, and live-in boyfriends and girlfriends. We see children living in one house for a few days with one set of stepbrothers and stepsisters and then in another home with a different group of stepbrothers and stepsisters. This can be very stressful for the adults involved, let alone the children. One of the reasons we have outlined a simple technique in this book is that parents no longer have a simple task. Often they have to parent other people's children as well as their own. The techniques we describe are meant to be used by all caretakers of children as a way of providing consistency and fairness. One of the best aspects of our technique is that it doesn't take a lot of time, though it does take thought and perseverance.

Parents, especially those who work outside the home, are often left with little time or energy for parenting. It is understandable that they turn to the television for help. While not encouraging their children to watch TV, they often passively capitulate to children's demands for TV. Children, of course, are drawn to the rousing stimulation of television. For a while it takes away their fear, anxiety, or sadness. Television, with its sounds and colors, is immediately rewarding. It makes kids feel temporarily better. Parents rightly feel that their children are addicted to TV. Children look to the television for relief from the cares of the day and to feel superficially better, something like alcoholics or drug addicts who look forward to their drug of choice. However, substituting the immediate excitement, that is, "television arousal," for sadness or anxiety does not take these negative feelings away. It only masks them for a short time. Children have to engage their feelings somehow or numb them out, burying them deep in their unconscious where they have a continued and uncertain affect on their psyche.

Parents lose control over their children quite easily. Let's look at a fairly typical example. John and Amanda are a middle-class couple—he a professional and she a homemaker. They are in their early 30s. Their 11-year marriage falls apart because John put his career over Amanda's needs. He didn't see that his two children were effectively without a father. Amanda and John divorced without much fighting and decided on joint custody of their six- and eight-year-old children. Now the children spend weekends with Dad and his girlfriend and her two children, and the rest of the week with Mom and her boyfriend. Their prospective stepfather is strict but caring. He demands that bedtime be carefully defined, and he is a stickler for manners. When the children are with their natural father, bedtimes are looser, and manners are not that important. The kids also have a difficult time adjusting to their stepfather in other respects. Their mother seems to be preoccupied with him, and they feel insecure. They focus on his need for rules. When they complain to their mother, she feels guilty and asks her boyfriend to ease up on the children until they get used to him. He had been criticized by his first wife for not being a "good" father. Now he feels hurt and slighted because he has been trying. He withdraws from the children, thinking he will let their mother handle the discipline. She feels hurt by his withdrawal, but wants to prove to him that her children can behave under a lighter hand. She begins to let them get away with things. "Why create a fuss and drive him further away by causing turmoil in the house?" she reasons. In a short time, she begins to lose control over her children, who are anxious and feel at sea in the first place. They start to dictate the rules to their mother. No one knows how to manage the children: the boyfriend has withdrawn, the mother has lost control, and the natural father and girlfriend see the kids for only short periods of time. Suddenly, the children are in control, and they are frightened. And the more frightened they become, the more in control they will demand to be.

Being the Boss So Your Child Can Be a Child

Whenever adults in charge of children are preoccupied with problems of their own or confused and divided on how to parent, a leadership vacuum occurs and children step in to fill the void. They take control of their lives and make decisions for themselves. Unfortunately, parents misunderstand this and sometimes encourage children to take responsibility for themselves and make their own decisions. This is a mistake, especially if the child is not old enough to handle full responsibility. Children need periods of what we call "age-appropriate carefreeness," during which they can explore and experiment with their world without the burden of responsibility. This is not to say that they shouldn't have *any* responsibility, but only as much as they can handle without stress.

Being the boss does not mean being a bully. Sometimes parents are the boss only to make their own lives easier. "Joan, go to your room and do your homework" might be translated by Joan as "I have to go to my room so my parents won't have to deal with me. They want me out of the way so they can have fun without me. They tell me it's for my own good to do my homework, but I know they don't want me around. They don't care about me. They enforce the rules when it suits them, and don't when it doesn't suit them." When children perceive their parents as using the rules and being the boss for their own sake and not for the children's sake, children begin to distrust authority figures and all rules. These children then become rule-breakers. Rules are seen by them as tools to benefit adults, not children, and therefore the children lose respect for both rules and adults.

Being the boss means making rules and sticking by them so children feel they are in a safe and predictable world. However, being the boss means making rules that work for the child as well as for the adult. The technique we describe in this book shows how parents can learn which rules are helpful and which are not. Having rules allows a child to feel, "Someone else is in charge. I can get on with being a child." Being a child means learning, having fun, and having periods of carefreeness. Children can relax and explore their world and learn in the process if they think someone in charge is looking out for them. Think about how much information a young child is taking in every day. New parents often report how quickly their child changes. Every month their child seems clearly different to them. During this period of rapid growth and change, children need stability and a feeling of safety that comes from knowing that someone they trust is the boss. They need to know that someone cares about them, understands their world and how they respond to it, knows how to live in it, and can protect them from serious mistakes and hidden dangers.

Some people might argue that parents who are the boss take away a child's initiative. "Don't children need to learn to be responsible for themselves?" is a question often asked of us. "Doesn't making mistakes teach a child how to deal with the problem next time?" Yes, but allowing children to make decisions before they are able to make wise ones is foolish. You don't ask a five-year-old if he would like to go to bed or stay up and watch television because most five-year-olds don't know what is best for them most of the time. If you allow children to make decisions before they are able to make wise ones, then they become frightened of making decisions. In fact, they become very dependent and want somebody else to make their decisions because they have made bad ones. Parents need to make rules that fit the child's needs, and stick to them until the child outgrows them with age and maturity. When a child has outgrown one set of rules, the rules can be changed.

Chapter 3

Why Punishment Doesn't Work

Punishment is not effective discipline. Punishment and discipline are not the same thing. To discipline means to teach. But punishment, as the dictionary points out, "is to subject a person to pain, loss, confinement, death, etc. as a *penalty* for some offense, transgression, or fault." Most importantly, punishment interferes with the trusting relationship that the parent and child must form.

Children make many mistakes in their choices and behaviors, so they need to be guided and helped. They need to be taught appropriate behavior. They *do* need discipline. They *do not* need punishment because punishments usually do more harm than good. Almost any punishment can snuff out an undesirable behavior if one scares a youngster enough, or hurts him, or uses force. The result is quick, but the effect is often short-lived. Only the negative side effects of punishment become well-entrenched in the child's personality.

Our Experience of Punishment

Punishment in its many forms is no stranger to any of us. It is still one of the most familiar experiences that we can relate to in our personal past and find in world history. Punishment is one of the oldest forms of social control known to humankind. Early educational guides in child rearing encouraged the use of punishment in ample doses. The schoolmaster used a dunce cap and a stick to "teach" his lessons and correct misbehavior. Unfortunately, the often misinterpreted Biblical statement, "Spare the rod and spoil the child," is probably the only disciplinary instruction some parents manage to remember. But in fact, this statement has much more to do with the consequences of a lack of true discipline than an endorsement of spankings with a stick.

Adults themselves are not exempt from punishment. We are reprimanded for inappropriate actions or mistakes, or penalized for breaking a law. We receive traffic tickets, have our licenses taken away, and may be sent to jail for certain infractions. Ingrained in the adult mind, consequently, is the belief that all wrongdoing should be punished. Over the years, psychiatrists, psychologists, educators, and other students of child development and human behavior have examined the effects of punishment on the individual. Those who dared question the long-range effectiveness of punishment were often misunderstood. Where fear and force were reduced or removed as goads to good behavior and before the value of better behavior was learned and internalized, confusion reigned and problems brewed. Small wonder that many returned to punishment in a panic to restore order. But students of human behavior continued to examine the effects of punishment on the individual, and though they followed different roads, they arrived at conclusions that were remarkably similar and are now generally accepted as fact.

Punishment can alter behavior, but the change that may be immediate is also usually temporary. If Michael pinches his provocative little brother and his mom spanks him for it and locks him in his room, he will not pinch his brother again, at least not while he is locked in his room. But he will probably pinch his little brother again when another provocation arises. Or, Michael will change his attack and slap his brother, since it was pinching that was punished, and after all, mom slaps. Michael learns to be sneaky and clever, not kind.

The driver ticketed for speeding will usually resume his old behavior within a few days, merely exerting greater vigilance for hidden speed traps. He has learned cunning, not safe driving. These changes in behavior tend to be temporary precisely because the individuals have not learned and incorporated the values in question. Their changes are simply a reaction to external force or pressure.

Once the threat of punishment is removed, the "bad" behavior often returns full strength. One has simply learned how to avoid punishment by choosing to misbehave when the authority figure is not around. This points out that force and fear do not direct children or adults toward learning the values of wiser, safer, more appropriate behaviors. The lesson and its value are not learned—and neither is the better behavior.

Many of us have experienced moments when we have punished or have been tempted to punish. We wish to use some harsh or violent treatment to "nip this action in the bud"—to "stop this behavior once and for all." We react with a punishment because we have allowed our own feelings of fear, anger, or impatience to flood us and overwhelm us. Parents who have made a habit of such seemingly shortcut techniques and wish to make some basic changes to improve their relationship with their children must learn to translate punishment into discipline.

The Long-Term Side Effects of Common Punishments

Punishments may stop a given misbehavior quickly (perhaps even permanently), but the consequences may cause a variety of seriously destructive side effects. The side effects may induce a whole new range of misbehaviors—including lying, stealing, cheating, shoplifting, or fire-setting. Or the side effects of harsh and unreasonable punishments may cause "internal injuries"—psychic scars or wounds that keep children from growing into happy, healthy, functioning adults. They may develop inhibitions, intense anxiety, phobias, night fears, bed-wetting, low self-esteem, neurotic guilt, fear of risk, anger turned inward, or anger and aggression turned toward all others. Punishment destroys child/parent relationships. It scars the psyche, fosters the sneak, and generates the bully.

Spanking is most commonly used in extreme situations, such as when a child runs into traffic or plays with fire. Spanking, happily, is being used less and less in families today, as parents and professionals realize that such physical punishments are painful, embarrassing, and fear-inducing experiences. Spanking in its variations—slapping, hitting, belting, beating—is rarely effective and always dangerous. The child retains more of a memory and resentment for the humiliation, pain, and fear inflicted in him than a clear memory of the lesson he was meant to learn. The parents who spank feel guilt that physical punishment has only estranged them from their child. They realize that as parents they have only discharged and relieved their own anger and fear through such punishment. Parents do not like to hurt their children, and they don't like to see that they have left their youngster sullen, devious, and rebellious as a result. Children who are physically punished learn that physical violence is a way to express frustration, fear, and disappointment. They learn to hit and bully others rather than to behave properly and learn the value of another person. That alone makes spanking a harmful, ineffective, and self-perpetuating punishment.

Withholding food, a previously earned reward, an allowance, or affection is another common punishment for misbehavior. Food is a powerful symbol of parental care and affection. When parents withhold meals, deny desserts, or even use foods as bribes, they start up a whole new tangle of eating and drinking problems for a child that can complicate his life well into adulthood.

Anthony gives his sister a swift kick under the table because she is "tattling" on him. For this double infraction, he is sent from the table by his exasperated mother. "No dessert," she says. So Anthony scuffs off to his room, feeling angry and mistreated. Later when his mother tries to re-establish a friendly relationship with him by offering him his chocolate pudding, Anthony refuses it with feigned disinterest to pay his mother back. Now his mom feels rejected and hurt. If Anthony doesn't like her dessert, Anthony doesn't like her. So she, too, withdraws into wounded silence.

Anthony has not learned to express his anger appropriately. His sister hasn't learned that tattling is wrong. His mother resorts to withholding sweets as a ticket to reaching him. Everyone is estranged and feeling bad because Anthony was punished rather than disciplined.

Isolation or banishment is commonly used as a punishment today. Parents are often encouraged to send their children to their bedrooms for "time out," or to "think about it" when they misbehave.

Amanda has been told by her papa to clear the dinner dishes from the table. With righteous indignation she states that this is an unfair request. It is her sister Jessica's turn. Amanda did the dishes last night, so she refused to obey her father's orders. Her father is angry with Amanda's disobedience and orders her to her room until she has decided to be obedient. Amanda marches out of the kitchen and up to her room, furious and determined not to give in to this unfair treatment. Amanda cannot survive in her room for the rest of her days being angry and thinking ugly thoughts—so only more unfairness is her lot. She has to "give in" to her father. Or, perhaps, her father has to "give in" to her?

We would say that their relationship is strained. One or the other of them could "give in" out of maturity. The father could relieve the situation by going to Amanda and kindly offering to discuss their differences and resolve their problem. It would have been easier if the father had protected their relationship by disciplining Amanda first for her disobedience and then dealing with Amanda's feelings about being unfairly treated.

Isolation or banishment of a child is an insidious and sometimes even malevolent form of punishment. Left alone with a wide range of feelings such as rage, worry, guilt, and shame, and thoughts of retaliation and revenge, a child feels abandoned and not at all certain there is anything left worth redeeming in themselves. When children misbehave they deserve the right to know that there are solutions to their behavior problems. They must know that they will not be abandoned or rejected or that their mistakes do not make them intrinsically bad or unworthy of love and help. They deserve to know that parents are a source of safety and solutions, and that they will offer comfort and security when things are in disarray. Stuffed animals and pets in a lonely bedroom cannot help them solve the situation.

Humiliation and hostile attacks destroy a child's self-confidence and self-esteem with devastating certainty. Ridicule and humiliation are sometimes used by parents as a form of punishment.

Ashley drops a dish she is wiping, and it breaks. Her father, preoccupied and irritated by problems at work, yells at her. He calls her a "fumbling, clumsy klutz" and instructs her to clean up "her mess" and "be more careful next time." Ashley is a normal, sensitive girl. Breaking the dish was an accident and not an intentional malicious act. Her father's words feel cruel and defining, and they only prove to her that she is clumsy. Why, she stumbled over Vince's feet in school yesterday. Yes, she must be a clumsy klutz. She feels dreadfully embarrassed and bad about who she is. She certainly does not think about wiping the dishes more carefully.

Repeated humiliations and serious ridicule will erode a child's self-esteem to the point where she will have few or no friends, do poorly in school, and be convinced that she is somehow a defective or bad person. She will lose interest in how she dresses or takes care of her things. She will feel defeated, give up easily, and criticize herself at the slightest provocation.

Defining a child with negative traits will only teach her to become what you define her to be. Parents don't like seeing their children reduced to such a fate. They enjoy watching a child grow to feeling good about themselves and about who they are.

Other nonpunishing parental tactics or responses to misbehaviors are sometimes used, but they are no more helpful in teaching children how to behave. *Threats* leave a child wondering which ones will come true and which ones won't. As threats are easier to make than to follow up on, the child soon learns to dismiss them and the parent as full of hot air, and to dismiss the parent as not being sincere. Creating overblown potential consequences to minor crimes only operates on the principle of fear and offers the child no alternative way of behaving.

Ignoring behaviors is the parents' way of avoiding issues that need serious attention consistently. Ambivalence in the parents' minds may be the cause of just "not noticing" what is going on. Misbehavior has to be taken seriously if you love your youngster. On the other hand, neither is one required to be "on the child's back" about every little thing.

Work as punishment spoils the joy a child can experience from doing a job well or from cooperating with others while doing a chore. To be sent back to pick up after oneself is certainly a reasonable consequence when a job is left unfinished. But to heap more work on what was already difficult to accomplish compounds the issue and offers no help.

Restrictions are easy to pronounce in a fit of frustration and are hard to enforce later on, so they usually break down early. "Two weeks of being grounded" or a "month of no TV" is usually a greater punishment for the parent to enforce than it is for the child to endure. Anger hangs in the air over both parties for too long and the child often knows that the parent will give in eventually.

Loss of privileges, like restrictions, is easier to invent than to enforce. To make a point about a bicycle being left in the rain once too often, locking the bike up in the garage for a short time may underline how serious you are about the issue. But it is important not to overdo the length of time you take the privilege away or else the child will remember the incident only as an injustice and not as the lesson you meant for him to learn.

Consequences to be faced squarely as the result of a mistake or lack in judgment are a good teacher to us all and certainly remain a part of all experiences. A child should not be protected from every unpleasant consequence he incurs. But as the only disciplinary tactic, waiting for the consequences of a behavior is not always practical. For example, the consequence of Justin not being able to get into his bed right away because of the mess in his bedroom could take a few weeks or more. On the other hand, the consequences of riding a skateboard in heavy traffic may never produce another opportunity from which to learn again.

The ultimate criterion for judging a disciplinary tactic is simple: Does it teach good behavior? As outlined in the preceding pages, although it's clear that punishment may temporarily or intermittently prevent bad behavior, it does not teach good behavior, and it does not help the child develop a conscience.

While defective in these primary purposes, punishment is remarkably effective and reliable in producing the following destructive secondary effects:

* It destroys parent/child relationships.
* It fosters the sneak and generates the bully.
* It causes anxiety and rage in the punished child and often in the punishing parent.
* It causes anxiety that actually interferes with the learning of the desired new behavior.

Most parents learn from their own experience what the behavioral scientists have discovered experimentally. Punishment does not teach good behavior effectively and has many destructive side effects.

To discipline is *not* to punish because to punish is *not* to teach.

Chapter 4

What Is Good Discipline?

Good behavior is learned, and it does not develop naturally. Children learn how to behave primarily from their parents but also from brothers, sisters, relatives, friends, neighbors, and teachers. To discipline means to teach, and it is the chief means by which parents can help their children learn good behavior. Hence, identifying those qualities which make one variety of discipline better than another is important. So, what is good discipline?

Good discipline is

- Immediate
- Consistent
- Certain
- Easily applied
- Fair
- Positive
- Appropriate in intensity
- Effective

Good discipline does not

* Leave unfinished business or loose ends
* Change the rules in the middle of the game
* Indulge in hollow threats and idle warnings
* Have to be severe
* Require heroic efforts to be effective
* Humiliate
* Hurt relationships
* Leave parent and/or child feeling bad about themselves

Good Discipline Is Immediate

When a child knows he has broken a rule he should, and usually does, feel guilty. But "feeling guilty" is useful only when it will help the offender change his ways as soon as possible. So the youngster need not be overwhelmed by guilt, nor should he spend a long time worrying about possible consequences. Prolonged anxiety serves no useful purpose. As soon as a parent is aware that her child has made a mistake, she must take it up with her child and discipline him. The child must learn that wrong or dangerous behaviors have consequences, at the least the consequence of a scolding. The mistake and the discipline must be strongly linked together.

Good Discipline Is Consistent

When parents ignore some mistakes and descend like avenging angels at other times, children become confused. If a toddler toys with the television controls and meets with approval or indifference on some occasions and is severely scolded on others, she is unsure of what she should do with all those enticing buttons.

A child is equally confused when one parent punishes a child for behavior that the other parent ignores or even encourages. Such inconsistencies teach the child that neither the parents nor their rules are to be trusted. Being consistent gives order and security to a child whose world looks chaotic and frightening at times. A predictable response allows the youngster the freedom to get on with life so she does not have to expend all of her energies exploring the extent of her boundaries and testing the sincerity of her parents.

To be consistent as a parent is not easy. Consistency implies a long-term commitment to the child, including a maturity about the responsibilities of raising him. It also takes energy. Mothers and fathers must agree on rules and help each other to be consistent. Divorced parents need to communicate effectively enough to teach agreement over issues that concern their children. Numerous picky rules are too hard to enforce consistently. So, it is wise to agree on rules that are vital and valuable, clear and age-appropriate. A lapse in consistency does not mean failure. Look for support. Try again.

Good Discipline Is Certain

Children are not impressed by idle threats and hollow warnings. They know exactly by the tone of your voice if you mean what you just said. Children will often break a rule if experience suggests you are ambivalent about this rule. In large part, the effectiveness of discipline is determined by its certainty and not its severity.

When children know beyond a shadow of a doubt that you mean what you say, they can internalize the rule, make it their own, and behave even when you are not there to check on them.

Good Discipline Is Easily Applied Almost Anywhere

We have already noted that if discipline is to be effective, it must be immediate, consistent, and absolutely certain. In turn, this means that any effective disciplinary strategy must also be reasonably easy to apply and be applicable almost anywhere. If it is not, the disciplinary strategy will be ineffective in that it simply will not be used at all. Being immediate, consistent, and certain in discipline is hard even for the best of parents, so good discipline had better be easy to apply under almost any conditions.

Good Discipline Is Fair

Very early in life, children develop an intense sense of justice. Most children know when they have made a mistake, and they tend to expect to be disciplined for that mistake. Though the response may range from mild reproach to a thundering scolding, the child needs to understand that he made a mistake and that discipline is a logical consequence of this faulty choice.

But some matters and rules are more important than others. Let's say a child accidentally spills a glass of milk across the dinner table and receives a harsh tongue-lashing, "Clumsy oaf! Every night we go through this . . . " Isn't a personal sense of worthiness far more valuable than a wet tablecloth? Given this response, the child will feel unfairly treated and diminished. However, if he is skateboarding down a busy street and is nearly hit by a car, his own sense of fairness will lead him to feel that stern discipline is in order and certainly fair.

Children who are disciplined unfairly do not learn from that discipline, and instead focus on their feelings of being treated unfairly. This defeats the purpose of discipline, which is to teach good behavior.

Good Discipline Is Positive

Nobody needs the lessons learned from negative discipline. The parent who humiliates his child or condemns her rather than the behavior does real damage. If, whenever she makes a mistake, little Nancy is told by her mother that she is a bad girl and someone who never does anything right, Nancy will, in time, come to believe that her mother is right. She will learn that lesson well. Her self-image will plummet, and her mother's angry words will become a self-fulfilling prophecy. She will become everything her mother called her. Simultaneously, her mother will feel unhappy and inept about her abilities as a parent.

Good discipline is positive. It offers help, a solution, and the promise of continued guidance and support. It does not leave the child without a solution. It does not diminish the child's identity and worth. It teaches good behavior in a way that rewards and reinforces the attachment between parent and child and leaves both feeling basically good about themselves and the other.

Good Discipline Is Appropriate In Intensity

Decent table manners are generally conceded to be desirable accomplishments. Yet few parents would seriously attempt to classify them as matters of life and death. A mother who "goes into orbit" when her Justin drops the juice pitcher will not be taken seriously by anybody nor does she deserve to be. Her son is not likely to have fewer accidents as a result of the rantings.

The inappropriate and excessive intensity of the mother's response has both discredited her in the eyes of her child and confused the child's sense of priorities. Imagine the decibel level this mother will have to reach when she reacts to Justin's tailgating experiments with his bicycle on the busy road! Tailgating is a life-threatening situation, and it would be appropriate to respond by "pulling out all the stops." We would want a child to learn this lesson once and for all because there may not be a second chance. An extremely intense response, presuming that it does not lapse into hysteria, is entirely appropriate for this mistake. So we save our "big guns" for the big issues and modulate our responses to smaller issues so that our reaction is appropriate to the "crime." Furthermore, intensity must be tailor-made to the degree of sensitivity of the child. Some children are very sensitive and don't require such highly charged responses. Others need an extra dose of intensity in order to be reached at all.

Good Discipline Is Effective

Remember, to discipline means to teach. This is the "bottom line," the ultimate criterion of good discipline: Does this or that disciplinary strategy actually teach good behavior?

Now, let's see if the One-Minute Scolding qualifies as a good disciplinary technique by examining it in the light of the criteria we have just identified.

The One-Minute Scolding Is Immediate

The One-Minute Scolding can and should be used as soon as the parent has recognized that the child has misbehaved or broken a rule. There is no need to wait because the One-Minute Scolding can take place anywhere and at any time. In ordinary circumstances, the child should be taken off privately so that the intense parent/child interaction, which is essential if the desired learning is to take place, will not be diluted by distractions such as the presence of onlookers or other interesting stimuli. However, there are times and circumstances when total privacy is not possible and scolding in front of others is entirely appropriate and can still be effective.

For instance, a parent may be driving on the freeway and her children continue to misbehave in the back seat despite several warnings. She drives off at the next exit, parks the car safely, and takes each offending child out of the car for an intense scolding in full view of the other occupants. These children will tend to obey Mom the next time she warns them in a similar circumstance.

The One-Minute Scolding Is Consistent

Being consistent is extremely important in any system of discipline. Yet, for most parents, consistency is a difficult goal to achieve. The One-Minute Scolding has a quick, ready-to-use formula that encourages parental consistency. It is easy to learn, reasonable, and will not induce unnecessary guilt. Hence, most of the "roadblocks" that prevent parents from being consistent have been removed. The One-Minute Scolding still requires a mature and responsible parent to consistently discipline a child, but herein lies the real reward of this discipline: The more you persevere, the sooner you will see the positive results of your efforts.

The One-Minute Scolding Is Certain

In this formula, there is no room for hollow threats or idle warnings. Dad clearly states that Jessica is to return promptly from the movies. A time has been set, and there is no ambivalence. If she is late, she will be disciplined. There is no hollow threat in this agreement. Her dad loves her. So he makes both the rule clear and the Scolding certain.

The One-Minute Scolding Is Easily Applied Almost Anywhere

The One-Minute Scolding can be extremely effective when whispered fiercely in the ear of a small child who refuses to behave in the supermarket and gently finished with a hug. Observers will silently, or perhaps not so silently, applaud that parent who has the courage and conviction to discipline a child in a public place. The child will learn that certain behaviors are not appropriate in supermarkets, restaurants, and other public places. Others being present will not be a protection from getting a scolding. The One-Minute Scolding can be used wherever it is needed.

The One-Minute Scolding Is Fair

Children do not like the One-Minute Scolding, but they admit that it is basically fair. They know that a One-Minute Scolding is the direct consequence of the bad behavior. They know they have made a mistake. They expect to be disciplined. They expect to be taught not to repeat that misbehavior. The timing and formula itself prevent an unfair dragging on of the process, or the inclusion of any additional restrictions.

The One-Minute Scolding Is Positive

In the first half of a One-Minute Scolding, a child is scolded for her misdeed. This part of the disciplining method is clearly stated. That the child has made a mistake is undeniable. However, the child is neither condemned nor put down for making a mistake. Rather, the child is told that the parent is angry, upset, or annoyed because the child chose to make that mistake. The child herself is never treated negatively—only her negative behavior is condemned.

Furthermore, the second half of the One-Minute Scolding allows the parent a good opportunity to be positive about her child and about their relationship.

"I love you. I think you are a fine person. You are a fine girl. You made a mistake, but I understand. You are going to learn how not to make that mistake and to choose the right behavior because I am going to help you. Every time you make a mistake, I'll remind you with a scolding. That's because I love you so much. That's why I discipline you, and I scold you." This is one of the most important aspects of the One-Minute Scolding because it provides a place for the loving affirmation of the child's unique identity and worth directly following an angry response to a misdeed. Personhood and behaviors do not cancel each other out. Anger and love do not negate each other.

The One-Minute Scolding Is Appropriate In Intensity

The intensity of the scolding and of the warm and caring feelings expressed in the second half of the lesson can be varied in intensity by the parent's good judgment. As parents become comfortable and at ease in using the One-Minute Scolding, they sharpen their ability to choose the intensity appropriate to the size of the misdeed as well as to the sensitivity of the child.

Very sensitive children (easily moved to tears with a mild scolding) need very much less intensity, or they remain anxious and fearful, always ready to flee from an angry parent.

Temperamentally hard-to-reach children, who have already developed a wall that does not admit feelings, need a very strong intensity level. The first half of the scolding where anger and frustration are expressed must be strong and penetrating. The second half of the scolding must be equally intense! Rib-cracking hugs, cheeks pinched, a tuft of hair tugged—it takes that kind of physical intensity to penetrate the defensiveness of some children because they would otherwise miss the feelings of intense affection they need to feel from you. Even when it does not come naturally, parents who are temperamentally soft, gentle, "laid-back," or overly relaxed have to learn how to relate with this kind of intensity.

The One-Minute Scolding Is Effective

After teaching the One-Minute Scolding for over twenty years to parents, teachers, and other family therapists, we have seen proof that it is a remarkably effective discipline. It teaches the child to expect uncomfortable consequences both of mistakes in judgment and in the breaking of family rules. It teaches the child by example how to deal with anger. It rewards the child for listening to the parent's explanation of what the mistake was and of the feelings it has caused in the parent. It clearly teaches the child what behavior is good and what behavior is not acceptable. It teaches the child that the parent cares for the child and wants to be a responsible, loving parent.

In our experience, when parents have used the One-Minute Scolding consistently and in the prescribed way, a marked improvement occurred in the behavior of the children very soon after the initiation of the method in nearly all cases.

Just as there are children who experience difficulty learning arithmetic and who need special help, there are also children who have difficulty learning how to behave appropriately and who require a longer period of consistent, frequent, and intense discipline—weeks or months. And there are those few who unfortunately require individual therapy and special programs that go beyond the capabilities of parentally administered One-Minute Scoldings (see Part III).

Chapter 5

How Conscience Develops in Children

Conscience is an important goal of all of our efforts at discipline. Far more important than re-establishing peace and quiet, or temporarily stopping offensive behavior, is the teaching of healthy behaviors and the values that underlie them. Parents hope that when their older children are left unsupervised, or have left home for the last time, they will ultimately become independent, and that they will function as happy and honorable members of a family and a community. In other words, parents hope that their children will have a *conscience*, one that includes both a sense of what is right and the will and conviction to follow it.

What is this conscience that parents want for their children? Most experts of human behavior would agree that it includes the following:

* The ability to behave honestly and to withstand temptation toward antisocial behavior

* The ability to defer immediate gratification for more distant rewards
* The ability to feel anxiety when considering misbehavior
* The ability to feel guilt or remorse after misbehaving

This combination of behaviors and feelings gives a person the tools necessary for behaving appropriately and living comfortably in society. The idea of conscience is neither old-fashioned nor outdated, despite the inclination of some to relegate it to the quaint environs of the Sunday school classroom. Quite the contrary, a developed conscience is essential to the health of both the individual and society. Its absence is evidenced in the symptoms of crime and violence. Children, adolescents, and adults with well-formed consciences rarely commit crimes.

Conscience does not just happen. It is taught to the child, directly and indirectly, by his parents and other significant persons, primarily in the first six or seven years of his life. The essential, nondispensable precondition for this teaching process we call conscience formation is a relationship of trust between a child and the teaching adult. A glance at how a child normally develops makes the reason for this readily understandable.

Normally, as the child grows, he associates security, warmth, and caring with his parents. They feed, nurture, and protect him. Although they are often a source of frustration to the child, parents are primarily felt as consistent and loving beings. Hence, without any significant need to erect barriers to protect himself from his parents, the child forms a loving bond with the parents and takes in their warmth and values.

Barriers to Conscience Formation

If, on the other hand, the relationship is troubled and conflicted, the intended messages of warmth, caring, and firmness may not be sent by the parent and/or received by the child. As a result, the child does not bond with the parent and does not take in the parent's values. Conscience formation does not occur.

Many factors may negatively affect both conscience formation and the trusting relationship between parent and child that must precede and accompany conscience development. Most of these factors can be grouped into three major categories:

* Parental problems
* Temperament of the child
* Fate

Parental Problems

Parents may be ineffective in forming a trusting relationship with their child for many reasons. One recent study (Glueck) followed potential delinquents from the age of two or three through the late adolescent years and found that two parental factors highly correlated with delinquency and poor conscience formation. Parents with serious mental illness, such as schizophrenia and alcoholism, or with a history of delinquency themselves, have a high percentage of children with delinquency. Preoccupied with their own emotional and psychological problems, they are unable to direct consistent efforts toward developing a close, trusting relationship with their child. The child may be seeking and be fully open to such a relationship with a parent who will teach him values and proper behaviors, but if the parent's attention is focused elsewhere, conscience formation will not occur.

For the same reason, parents with troubled marriages have difficulty creating the warm, secure family environment that is the precondition for the transmission of values to their children. Their energies are diverted from child care and instruction to coping with problems in the marriage relationship. The same may be said of parents struggling with work, physical health, and alcohol or drug problems.

Another common, but poorly understood, factor that seems to interfere with conscience formation arises when the parent teaches the child to turn to himself when in trouble or need. For whatever reason, be it parental disinterest, incompetence, or ideology, the child is taught to seek his own solutions to moral issues and to expect neither parental nor societal guidance in making certain choices. For instance, he learns that lying is easier than telling the truth. Whenever he turns to his parents or to others for guidance and instruction, he receives either no input or their smiling confidence that he can handle the problem alone. Inevitably, he comes to perceive his parents as distant and even weak, and he fears that they may not be strong enough to help him with his fears and difficulties. Frustrated in his need for guidance and instruction, he is at the same time afraid to express his fear and rage because to do so may drive these weak parents even further away. Feeling essentially alone and unprotected in a frightening world, he sets out to create a "safe place" for himself by controlling and manipulating every aspect of his environment, including his parents. He becomes "the observer," and not a participant, not the one responsible for making his own choices and mistakes.

Aided only by his expanding ability to manipulate and control his environment, the child is compelled to use every bit of his psychic energy and skill to prevent further abandonment by his parents. He recognizes that his intense feelings of fear and rage might interfere with vigilance and thus his ability to control and manipulate the environment. So he learns to "numb out" these and most other feelings. In time, this child becomes unteachable. He is distant and emotionally unavailable to his parents. Hence, any ethical formation that occurs in him is strictly intellectual and thus fragile and susceptible to collapse under even moderate pressure. It lacks the deep grounding in experience necessary to support moral values under pressure. As a result, even modest temptation may be sufficient to radically alter the choices he makes. In any case, his sole preoccupation is survival: he must control and manipulate his environment in any fashion necessary to guarantee that nothing can cause him injury or harm.

Even when parents are clear and consistent about their own values, they may not be aware of their child's need for explicit direction. For example, when Christopher is angry with his sister, he hits her. Although his parents may hold it as a value that children work out their own problems, they need to teach Christopher that there are more appropriate ways to express his feelings.

Parents with unconscious conflicts about obeying authority may subtly encourage their child to disobey laws. While paying lip service to the prevailing authority, they may smile quietly and give emotional support to their child when he chooses to disobey. The child is sent conflicting messages about the proper way to respond to a rule: overtly, he is taught to obey the law, but covertly, through the power of his parents' repressed feelings, he is told to disobey.

An unusually malignant injury is inflicted when one parent unconsciously encourages a child to disobey the family rules in order to antagonize or hurt the other parent. For example, a father may unconsciously reward some of his daughter's behaviors which are particularly upsetting to her mother. If this pattern persists, the child will tend to disdain her parents and scorn their rules as a means of coping with life's problems.

Some parents insist on very high standards for their children's behavior, and then not only do they fail to discipline them for their mistakes, but they actually reward them for their misbehaviors by showing excited interest in what their children have just done. This significantly interferes with conscience formation and, worse still, seems to elicit defiant and antisocial behavior from the child. For example, a mother harangues her fifteen-year-old daughter, Julia, forbidding her to date an eighteen-year-old boyfriend. Yet when Julia defies her mother and comes home from an outing with the forbidden boyfriend, not only does the mother fail to discipline her, but instead she displays interest and curiosity about the date. Julia is confused and angered by her mother's double message.

This parental mistake is fairly common and inevitably forces the child to act contrary to the parent's *conscious* wishes. The child obeys her parent's *unconscious* demand that she misbehave.

Parents who say one thing and do another confuse and anger their children. Joseph observes his father laughing and joking about stealing expensive tools and supplies from his employer. At the same time, Joseph receives regular admonitions from his father to be honest and respect the property of others. Indeed, he is severely punished for swiping candy from the corner drugstore. Such a conflict between his father's words and deeds is bound to generate anxiety, disappointment, and confusion in Joseph. It will certainly not assist in the development of any clear commitment to the virtue of honesty. In an environment where no explicit parental orders or rules have been given on a specific subject, a bad example by a parent can have a powerful negative effect on conscience development. The perpetually drunken parent, though regularly contrite and apologetic after each binge, leaves his child with uncertainty about the appropriate use of alcohol. The parent also renders himself less available and less competent as a trusted teacher of values and appropriate behavior. It is highly unlikely that a child will turn to an alcoholic parent when in need.

Parents who try to teach their children by using only one level or an inappropriate level of feeling expression, whether of high or low intensity, are handicapped by their inability to teach values and to form their child's conscience. Matthew "forgets" to take out the garbage and gets a mild rebuke from his father. When Matthew takes money from his grandmother's purse, and his father gives him the same kind of mild rebuke, Matthew does not learn that there is a difference in severity of the two misdeeds. One mistake feels no different from the other. Samantha, for example, complains that her mother yells at her all the time. Whether she "forgets" to make her bed before leaving for school, or whether she comes home two hours late from a date, her mother's response is the same high-pitched, intense yelling.

Both Matthew and Samantha are receiving confusing messages on different levels. They are left in doubt about the relative importance of two apparently unequal acts. The parents' pattern of giving similar responses to very dissimilar behaviors calls into question the depth of their commitment to the children.

If the parent hopes to give the child a well-ordered hierarchy of values, the *intensity* of his response to the child's behavior must reflect the place of a specific behavior in the total hierarchy of values. On his way to school, Ed comes upon a friend in distress and in need of help. He has been taught by his parents to be at school on time *and* to help people in distress. Ed will almost certainly make his choice on the basis of which value, punctuality or helping your neighbor, has been taught with the most intensity by his parents.

Unavailability of a parent for establishing a trusting relationship with a child, unwillingness or inability to teach with clarity and honesty, and/or an inconsistency between parental words and deeds, will all effectively prevent a child from forming an adequate conscience. If parents want their children to develop a strong and effective conscience, they must teach effectively. For good or for evil, the combination of what they say and what they do will teach their children the values, feelings, and behaviors that together constitute conscience. If they have created a trusting, un-conflicted relationship with their child, and if their own lives are reasonably consistent with their words of instruction, they will have done all parents can do to help their child form a conscience.

The Child's Temperament

Parental problems are not the only factors that interfere with conscience formation. A child may be born with a temperament that interferes with the development of a trusting relationship with his parents.

Difficult-to-Raise Children

In their study of delinquent adolescents, the Gluecks found that when these delinquents were two or three years old, they were commonly described as nonsubmissive to authority, destructive, extremely restless, defiant, and stubborn.

Chess and Thomas identified a group of children (about ten percent of the total) which they labeled "difficult-to-raise." These children had very irregular biorhythms and experienced great difficulty establishing regular sleeping, eating, and elimination patterns. One night, they would sleep the whole night through. The next night, they would awaken two or three times. They had irregular eating needs. During one 24-hour period, they might eat much more than the next 24 hours. These "difficult" children also tended to respond to new experiences in a negative way, usually by withdrawing. When presented with "new" foods, they rejected or refused to eat them until repeated presentation allowed the food to become familiar.

During periods in life when new experiences are few, the child's temperament might appear to have changed. For example, after accepting the new experience of toilet training, a child's temperament might become calmer. However, when faced with the major new experience of school three years later, the child's underlying temperament might manifest itself again in the form of fear, anger, stubbornness, or other tactics aimed at avoidance of a new experience.

These "difficult" children tend to have intensely negative moods. They cry more than they laugh. They fuss more easily than they express pleasure. They are not wholly unadaptive, but simply are very slow to adjust to new situations.

While neither dull nor unresponsive, many of these children exhibit a lack of sensitivity to their environment, particularly their human environment. Paradoxically, such children may be hyper-active and seem over-responsive to their environment. However, what we actually see is their attempt to engage their environment in such a way so as to obtain an intense response. These children seem to require a highly stimulating and exciting environment, without which they feel alienated and lonely. If their parents are not unusually intense and stimulating, they are perceived as dis-tant, unavailable, and weak.

Nurturing such children is a demanding and stressful task. Most parents feel that their love and acceptance should transform them into happy and contented children. When the desired transformation fails to materialize, they blame themselves, feeling guilty, anxious, and helpless. Often, these parents become so frustrated and distressed by their experiences that they turn their anger toward each other, or withdraw almost completely from their child. Most children respond initially to parental withdrawal by increasing their level of protest, which in turn elicits further parental withdrawal. Eventually, the children too give up and resign themselves to alienated and lonely lives.

Parents who have one of these "difficult" children hope that school and perhaps a good peer group will help their child. However, they discover that he also has trouble learning and behaving in school. He does not learn how to make or keep friends. He continues to have a troubled relationship with his parents and therefore his conscience tends to be weak and ineffective. He does not learn the rules, values, and feelings that would help him to relate to friends, family, and others. He feels alienated and alone, and he views his parents as weak and distant, unable to provide him with a safe relationship within which he can relax. He tests other adults who supposedly have authority over his behavior, and he learns that he can manipulate them, too. Teachers, principals, social workers, police, and judges all become enemies who have proven themselves unable to control him and are consequently unworthy of his trust and respect.

Because these children need intense stimulation before they feel alive and in contact with others, they tend to seek excitement, thrills, and danger. These experiences allow them to "numb out" their feelings of sadness, loneliness, and alienation. Without the help of a strong conscience, they drift inexorably toward delinquency, violence, and crime. Fortunately, only a small percentage of children are born with this temperament. Most are born with a temperament that easily allows the development of a good, strong conscience.

The Overly Sensitive Child

At the other end of the spectrum are those overly sensitive children who are highly vulnerable to the influence of their parents. If their parents provide a secure, predictable environment, teaching values and behaviors in an unconflicted manner, these children develop a conscience that is a helpful guide to them in their daily lives. They can relate to people in authority without fear, and they know the rules of family, school, and community. They have the tools that enable them to work and play in the different social structures within which they must function.

However, these sensitive children develop significant problems if their parents and teachers are unaware of their specific difficulty or are unwilling to adjust their parenting to their child's particular needs. Such children tend to be too easily affected by their parents. If the parent is unconsciously hostile, the child will accept her parent's feelings about herself and will perceive herself as loathsome or unlikable.

The child with such a sensitive temperament learns her lessons too well. A single harsh "no" from a parent becomes a commandment. The child soon has learned so many "no's" that she walks a very narrow and tortuous line. Her life may become an ordeal, avoiding all those prohibited thoughts and behaviors. Dirt, noise, excitement, touching, feeling—all this becomes suspect. The child becomes fearful of her own ideas and desires. She feels there is no safe place and perhaps no safe relationship. Her conscience becomes a monster. She refuses to risk and is constantly anxious, fearful that unless she is eternally vigilant, something terrible will unexpectedly occur. Her conscience demands constant anxiety. Every situation, and every person is potentially dangerous. She cannot relax. She cannot relate. Her life is an unending ordeal. Her conscience is not helpful. Indeed, it burdens her until there is little or no joy in her life.

Parents who find themselves with children who are temperamentally oversensitive to the important persons in their lives must adapt their own parenting styles to the specific needs of these children. Unless their parents recognize their unique needs and provide the special parenting they require to develop a strong but non-punitive conscience, these children are likely to form inhibiting or punishing consciences.

Fate

An increasing number of children in our society have experienced enough painful trauma that they have difficulty trusting even the best of parents or other adults, and therefore have difficulty forming a strong conscience. Very common among these are the children who have suffered the loss of a parent at an early age. Divorce or the death of a parent is a particularly painful experience for a small child. When one loved parent inexplicably leaves a child and his family, the child suffers a profound loss and may fear abandonment or loss of the remaining parent. If Mom has to work outside the home because of divorce and has to place her child with a baby-sitter or in a day-care center, the child "loses" mother, too. Clinging, whining, and downright panic become very common in such children. The child's whole attention is directed toward avoiding the loss of his mother and is thus diverted from his proper task of learning how to behave and feel in social situations.

Children who have been mistreated, neglected, or abandoned, either physically or emotionally, feel enraged because of the mistreatment, but they also experience the fear that the mistreatment or abandonment may recur. Even when placed with "good" parents who have proven themselves capable of forming strong parent/child bonds, these children have serious difficulties trusting and forming an effective conscience. They are preoccupied with emotional and physical survival in a hostile world. The niceties of conscience formation pass them by with barely a flicker of interest.

The Art of Creating a Conscience

We have examined the difficulties underlying the teaching and learning of conscience. We have seen the circumstances in which conscience formation fails, and we have noted that a trusting relationship between parent and child is essential for successful conscience formation. How do parents establish such a relationship if trust does not exist? How do they capture a temperamentally distant and manipulative child and stuff an unwanted conscience inside? How do they repair the devastation of a painful loss so that their child is receptive to their care and instruction?

Growth, change, and development are basic to a child. Children are programmed for change. There are very few children who cannot develop a trusting relationship with a parent if that parent is determined to succeed. Even the most difficult child can learn how to behave and how to feel the guilt and remorse necessary for building a conscience. The pain and anguish of a loss can be relieved by parents who can empathize and engage those feelings that interfere with learning the lessons of conscience formation. Parents can and must teach their children to trust, to feel, and to behave.

The Role of the One-Minute Scolding

Discipline is the most intense, explicit, and successful form of teaching conscience. As we have learned, an approach to discipline must have certain characteristics in order to be successful. The One-Minute Scolding is an effective discipline because it focuses on the development of a trusting relationship. It compels both parent and child to engage in that process we call relating, bonding, or attachment. Firm, consistent, kind, and intense discipline can be the beginning and the foundation of a trusting parent-child relationship and the formation of a strong conscience. Because it both depends upon and promises an intense, trusting relationship, the One-Minute Scolding must be given by a significant adult. Ordinarily, only parents or parent substitutes can promise a child such a relationship. Teachers, probation officers, and counselors can be helpful and supportive to their pupils and charges, but they cannot promise these children an enduring and trusting relationship.

The One-Minute Scolding is not a panacea. It will not cure troubled parents or resolve marriage problems. It alone will not make a child happy or secure in his new foster home. However, the One-Minute Scolding is a simple way to begin a new discipline and a new relationship, and it seems to work despite parental problems. The One-Minute Scolding is an effective discipline *if it is used*.

The simplicity of the One-Minute Scolding and its easy applicability to most disciplinary situations allows even the most troubled parent to use it successfully. Indifferent or troubled parents may have difficulty initiating the One-Minute Scolding because their child's needs may not be uppermost in their minds. These parents will require much encouragement and support from their friends and other adults to begin and persevere in their discipline. Our experience with troubled parents has convinced us that they can and will use the One-Minute Scolding as effective discipline for their children if given adequate direction and encouragement. If they can be encouraged and supported to use the One-Minute Scolding in a friendly and consistent manner, they are invariably rewarded by significant and almost immediate improvement in their child's behavior. Often, troubled parents have few pleasures or successes in their lives and they find success with their children particularly rewarding. Their marriage may have failed, and they may feel overwhelmed by their problems, but when their stubborn three-year-old responds to them positively, their life becomes much more pleasant.

Parents who give their children conflicting messages as to what is right and what is wrong must resolve these conflicts before they use the One-Minute Scolding. Parents need to agree on what is proper behavior and what is not. A child does not need numerous rules—only a few explicit and clear-cut commands are required. When a child misbehaves, he must be confronted with the mistake in a kind but firm manner. Both of the parents and the child must all know what is a mistake, and what is not. Both parents must be willing to discipline their child when he needs discipline. He needs discipline (teaching) whenever he breaks a rule.

There is nothing magical about the One-Minute Scolding. If one parent uses it to discipline her child for misbehaving, and the other parent unconsciously rewards the child for the same behavior, the child will still be confused as to what his parents want him to learn.

Using the One-Minute Scolding with Difficult-to-Raise Children

For children who have developed an "internal barrier" to the feelings of others, the One-Minute Scolding is the most effective, and in some cases, the only effective discipline. Children who have been taught to rely on themselves for help and children born with the "difficult-to-raise" temperament have "numbed out" their own feelings and in the same process have become insensitive to the feelings of others. These children require intense expressions of feelings from the disciplining parent to penetrate their "feeling barrier." Such scoldings must not be too long or the child will have time to marshal his defenses and keep the parent and the parent's feelings at a distance. Immediately after the short, intense scolding, the parent dramatically relaxes and becomes tender and loving. In that brief moment when the child's psyche scrambles to adjust to the different parental message, the warmth and caring of the parent floods the child.

Initially, the child manages to distance herself quickly from the parent's loving words and attention. She is suspicious and guarded, suspecting some sort of trickery. As the child experiences more and more disciplining over the weeks and months, she gradually allows more and more of the warmth and caring of the parent to touch her. As she opens to the parent's love, she is better able to learn the lesson. Though the child may not put her thoughts into words, even to herself, nevertheless she moves through an internal process which goes something like this:

"Mother gets angry when I disobey her. She reminds me every time I forget to obey her. She also tells me how much she loves me, and she tells me nice things about myself. I love my mother. I don't want to make her angry."

These children can respond and change their behavior quickly. However, their conscience development is slow and uneven, even with the consistent use of the One-Minute Scolding. They tend to be "flexible" and may appear to be compliant and docile when confronted by parents who are using a new and unfamiliar discipline. However, several months of consistent discipline will be necessary before signs of conscience are regularly seen. Children who have been neglected and mistreated, especially those who have been "abandoned" several times, seem to respond to the One-Minute Scolding when they don't respond to any other discipline. The conscience of such a child has not developed because the child has put all of his energy and abilities into protecting himself from further mistreatment or another abandonment. He does not trust his parents. Values and behaviors can be adopted if they seem to protect him from danger or loss. But they will be just as easily abandoned if they seem no longer useful in preventing pain or loss.

These children feel alone and alienated. They have great difficulty *feeling* the parent's love and concern. They can hear conscience-forming messages from the parents, but they attach very little feeling to them. In such children, conscience formation can occur only when the parent delivers the message with great intensity of feeling and then rewards the child for listening with equally intense expressions of tenderness and caring. The parents must use their bodies, particularly their hands, to express these feelings to the child. In the first half of the scolding, they communicate their intense feelings of anger using their face, body, and gestures as well as their words. They then touch, stroke, and hug their child, telling him also through body language that they care deeply for him. Few children can resist long if the parents repeatedly engage them in this attachment process.

Children who are temperamentally insensitive to their human environment, as well as children who have had parents with a single level of feeling-response to their misbehaviors, respond well to the One-Minute Scolding if it is given with appropriate feeling by the parents. Temperamentally insensitive children absolutely require scoldings that begin with an intense discharge of the parent's feelings.

"I am so angry with you, I could grind you to powder!"

The child must *feel* his parent's feelings so that his focus of attention is narrowed and directed toward that parent. He must not be allowed to distance himself and observe. When the feelings of the parent dramatically change, the child is remarkably vulnerable and open to them. The parent rewards the child with love and tenderness. The rule, the limit, and the value enter the child's memory along with the warmth and tenderness. Conscience formation progresses slowly but surely.

Using the One-Minute Scolding with Sensitive Children

The One-Minute Scolding can also be used quite effectively with overly sensitive children, but their parents need to remember that their strong feelings have a very powerful impact on this child. These parents must modulate their feelings to a level that will not overwhelm their child. A shorter scolding time with less intense feelings, but with very clear and consistent messages, will facilitate the development of a very adequate conscience in these children.

Tracking Conscience Development in Our Children

What do parents look for in children as signs of conscience formation? In the first stage, they will detect that the child knows he has made a mistake, that he is aware of what is right and what is wrong. However, he may not yet be anxious about the wrongness of the deed so much as worried about the possibility of getting caught.

In the next stage, parents will notice that their child not only knows when he makes a mistake, but he feels bad about it as well. Guilty behavior and remorse now are likely to follow a misdeed and, in general, a marked decrease in misbehaviors should become evident over an extended period of time. Unfortunately, this is the stage of conscience formation when many parents relax and turn their attention to other, perhaps more urgent matters. They are not aware that their child's conscience remains fragile at this stage and that they must continue to devote time and energy to their child's developing conscience.

In the next phase of conscience formation, parents will notice that their child has become aware that his behavior affects the trusting relationship he has with them. No longer does the child fear only his parent's punitive response to his mistakes, he is *aware* and *regrets* that his behavior has an affect on their relationship.

"When I hit my little sister, my Mommy gets mad. When Mommy gets mad, I get scared. She might go away!"

Parents may see the child's attempt to restore his relationship with them. He may ask for forgiveness or do something that will please or placate them. He fears their displeasure and is aware that his misdeed has caused the loss of the important feeling of security and trust that should characterize all parent-child relationships.

Finally, when conscience formation is well advanced, the parents may note that the child becomes anxious at just the thought of committing a forbidden act. His conscience has expanded beyond simply knowing what is right and wrong and that his parents will become upset with him if he misbehaves. Now, when he makes a mistake, he experiences an inner sense of *estrangement from his idea of who he is:* "I'm not the sort of person who does that kind of thing."

The child's relationship to his parents has developed so that he feels close to them, and he no longer fears that he has no one to turn to when in need. When faced with a moral problem, he recalls the teaching of his parents and their feelings about similar problems he has encountered in the past. He may compare his anticipated behavior with his own expectations of himself. He is motivated not only by a fear of losing the trusting relationship he now has with his parents but also by a true sense of what is right. He also has a sense that he is a person who does the right thing.

Conscience formation is a matter of critical importance for the individual, the family, and society. It is a long-term process of teaching by the parent, based upon a trusting relationship between parent and child. Effective and consistent discipline is a vital component of that teaching. The One-Minute Scolding is a particularly effective discipline for troubled children and parents because it not only disciplines, but it also engages both parent and child in the development of a trusting relationship—the root of a healthy conscience.

Chapter 6

The Importance of Saying "No"

We talk so often of being positive. We even speak of the One-Minute Scolding as being "positive discipline," but the One-Minute Scolding does have its negative side—its angry, negative feeling side. What is good about the One-Minute Scolding is the fact that it is whole, complete, and, though it is discipline, it ends with positive feelings. It is positive in its net effect. It affirms the child. It is this balance of positive and negative that is critical.

Coming to Terms with "No"

Today many people feel very uncomfortable with negative feelings, especially with anger, and they have trouble expressing them. We are so afraid to hear the negative or to be negative that saying a clear, crisp "no" seems impossible. "Will you volunteer to work on the school auction?" "Well, let me see, I'd really love to, but I'm not sure I'm free . . . "

Adults have difficulty saying "no" to each other. They fear engaging the finality of "no." They'll whip up a froth of angry commentary that leads to nothing when what they really want to say is "no." Even among themselves, adults must learn to give a "no" honestly and clearly and to accept "no," perhaps not joyfully but certainly as a reality.

A wife will contract the proverbial headache rather than say "no" to her husband's sexual wishes. She actually takes on pain in her fear of giving pain. She defines her husband as too weak to fully engage her current reality and deals him a blow by not allowing him the chance to be strong enough to hear her clear and honest "no."

Somewhere in Between

"Mommy thinks you'd better stop playing in the sand now. She wants you to have your bath. If you don't come in soon . . . " "You've got to accentuate the positive, eliminate the negative, latch on to the affirmative . . . " But by eliminating the negative, we've actually created "Mr. In-between."

"No" is a word with rights equal to "yes." Its meaning is different, but its value is utterly equal to that positive word "yes."

Two-year-olds have none of this prejudice. They can say "no" with authority. This word is useful to them. It is the ultimate expression of their budding autonomy, and mothers hate it. We call that stage the "terrible twos." It is that time when mother and child are thrust into opposite camps. Does emancipation have to be won? Certainly. But does so much of it have to be filled with anger, fear, and danger? Imagine if parents came to enjoy that early symbolic gesture of autonomy in their toddlers? What might happen if "no" lost its battle cry status and became a word, used first by the parent with the same authority and definition but without anger? What if "no" lost its association with fear, anger, ambivalence, or anxiety?

While grandma's house may abound with "no-no's"—the Boston fern, the trinkets on the coffee table, the stair railings, and the detergents under the sink—at home, "no" can be centered on a few, easy-to-apply areas.

Teaching "No" as a Part of Life

"No" is a legitimate, negative fact of life, so it can be taught with validity and need not be filled with anger or fear. "No" can become a game in which the parent teaches the negative facts of life with certainty. "No" can be slow and gentle; it can be laughed and sung, and chuckled and danced. It can be loving, and it can be associated with the joy and concern of a parent who denies dangers to the child. But it is still a clear and unambivalent "no." A woman said, "I'd hate to have an adult walk in and hear the nonsense songs I sing to my son. One day after lunch I found myself having to wash his face. He *hates* being washed. So I did this operatic farce and playfully insisted on what had to be done:

"O.K., Charlie, time to wash the squash from your face. Here comes the washcloth."

"No! No! No!"

"No! No! Wash the squash."

"No, we wash a lot."

"No, squish, no squash."

"No, mish, no mash."

"Behold Charlie! I can see your shining face again!"

Because "no" has gotten such bad press, parents often fear that "no" is associated with "being a witch," or being stingy and withholding. This mixed feeling creates ambivalence in a parent's tone of voice when they have to say "no."

Another mother said, "I hate saying 'no' to my children so much. I know how important it is not to be ambivalent, so I drown out my wish to say 'yes' only to find myself barking my no like a crack drill sergeant. Then I forbid them to react to me with disappointment or dismay. I just don't want to hear about it."

But that is what a mature parent needs: the ability to say "no" and accept the angry disappointment of a denied youngster. If the "no" has been unambivalent, children will know it, and the disappointment will probably be short-lived. If they detect a glimmer of ambivalence or mixed feelings in your voice, they will play their anger and disappointment to the hilt to see if they can drive a wedge into your denial.

Certain children find that it is difficult to know if your "no" is final. They hear your "no" as if it had been whispered from across the Grand Canyon. For them, you must express your "no" as intensely as is needed so there is no doubt that you mean what you say. When you really don't know if you need a "no" or a "yes" in a given situation, it's perfectly correct to delay the answer with an honest, "You know, I'm not sure, let me think about it, and I'll tell you by such-and-such a time."

Balancing "No" and "Yes" Between Parents

"No" as a word is "worse" than "yes" only when used disproportionately. "No" has rights equal to "yes."

"Opposites attract," they say, but even so, parents often juggle their feelings and attitudes between themselves early on in a marriage, with one partner taking on a generally pessimistic attitude and the other partner upholding the positive. Indeed, between themselves they balance and augment each other's viewpoints and responses. But eventually that balance ceases to work. The pessimist, for instance, can become so unrealistic and negative that the optimist leaps too quickly to a positive position that is equally unrealistic. The two have developed a gap in the middle, and their true values fall through the gap and get lost. The two no longer help each other as partners but only react to each other. Living only "one role" can eventually become divisive.

A woman says, "I hate riding the broom in my house all the time! My husband is so positive and permissive with the kids without seeming to consider the prices or possible consequences of his generous permission. That makes me feel, first, aced out of an equal share in the decision-making process. Second, I feel bereft of the opportunity to be the positive and giving person I used to see myself as being. And, third, I get stuck with the consequences and the follow-through of his generous gestures because I'm with the children more than he is. Now the kids go to him for his inevitable yesses, and I've become the witch who doles out 'Nos.' Saturday he took them out for ice cream, not knowing that I had already told them that we were going to have to wash the car together."

Here "no" has become the sole right of one partner and "yes" the privilege of the other. As each person in the partnership wants to grow to a balanced, and responsible wholeness within himself or herself, they feel uncomfortable bearing only one side of the message. Trading seats on the seesaw is not a long-term solution, although initially trading places may be necessary to wrench themselves out of the habits or patterns they have already formed. Whenever one partner is enlightened and ready for a new developmental step toward wholeness and takes some first steps in that direction, the balance between partners becomes shaky and precarious. That's not bad, but it is unsettling and often painful.

The mother speaking above needs to see why she's been so comfortable riding that broom of hers for so long. She has every right to pick up the whole tab and speak from her deepest self—stating a "yes" or a "no"—and not just reacting to her husband out of a need to make balance. She needs to talk this out with her spouse and tell him how she feels. She needs to be clear enough to know her own mind. She might create some "yes is the answer" situations artificially for a while just to park her broom in the corner for a time and practice the joys of saying "yes" to her youngsters. Her husband might check out his motives to see if he fears saying "no" because he is not strong enough to withstand his youngsters' disappointments or some bouts with "unpopularity." The tensions between "yes" and "no" are superseded when each partner knows himself clearly enough to speak out both answers with authenticity, joy, and authority.

The One-Minute Scolding is a great arena for both parents to grapple with and express positive and negative realities fully and wholly. If "no" is the word a two-year-old uses with the daring of one who has discovered his key to autonomy, then "no" or a fascination for the forbidden is a major issue once again in adolescence. When parents come to understand the two sides of the truth in a two-year-old's rebellion, they recognize that "no" is a healthy child's attempt to separate. They acknowledge and applaud the child's separation, but at the same time they protect him from "delusions of grandeur." Children must not leap from the role of helpless babe to almighty dictator! The successful accomplishments of "the terrible twos" will stand one in good stead when as an adolescent the child intensifies his emancipatory efforts.

Saying "No" to Your Teenager

A factor that plays an important part in parenting a teenager is just how well the parent survived his/her own adolescence. How much autonomy did the parent attain at that time?

The experiences the parents had as adolescents affect their efforts to parent their teenagers. They may decide to imitate their parents or they may choose to do the opposite as a reaction to what they perceive to be a painful adolescence. If parents differ in their expectations, limits, and responses to their teenager, the youth will be confused and troubled. One parent may have unconscious feelings and agendas that powerfully push the adolescent toward maladaptive behaviors. Fortunately, the teenager is subjected to a number of influences that tend to mitigate the noxious effects of one troubled parent or an anti-social friend. Societal norms, school rules and regulations, church expectations, peer pressure, and extended family all influence the choices and behaviors of the adolescent.

Consciousness and clarity are again imperative in saying "yes" or "no." Goals and values must be clear: Say what you mean and mean what you say.

"Mother, may I go out to swim?"

"Yes, my darling daughter. Hang your clothes on the hickory limb, but don't go near the water."

This mother says "yes," but means "no."

Another mother tells her 15-year-old daughter, "You may not sleep with your boyfriend, but if you are going to, I'll put you on the pill." Or, if she forbids her daughter to have sexual intercourse with her boyfriend but does not set clear guidelines about when to be home, how often they may go out, and does not enforce these limits clearly, firmly, and lovingly, then she has said "no," but means "yes."

The story of the forbidden fruit in the Garden of Eden deals with the problem of "no." This is a paradigm of the emancipation issue. Every paradise has its forbidden fruit. At first one is forbidden the fruit, but by adolescence one is faced with the serpent itself. Eventually one eats of the fruit and tastes as never before "the knowledge of good and evil." This knowledge casts us from the bliss of ignorance into another reality. Here enter the tensions of knowing good from evil, the problem of choosing for ourselves between "yes" and "no." Guilt and vulnerability, shouldered and accepted, allow us to pick up our bags and walk into adulthood, choosing between the two, paying the prices incurred by this choice, and experiencing the joys offered by that choice. God himself says in effect, "You blew it, but I love you and I'm going to help you."

Deep down, parents sense that it is ultimately necessary for their children to disobey that "no" in order to emancipate. And saying "no" to one's parents is an act of emancipation. For example, if the parents insist that their 17-year-old son abide by a curfew of 9 p.m. on a weekend, the youth should respond with a confident "no." On the other hand, this is not the case for a 13-year-old. Small wonder that "no" is filled with such feeling and ambivalence. It represents both freedoms for our children and the loss of them.

Our children's emancipation will succeed only when the rules and values we have imparted to them have been clear and firm enough to push off from. Emancipation will succeed only when the child is mature enough to cope with the consequences of his choices. Hence, parents must create a formative setting for their children in such a way that they can obey until they are strong enough to disobey. Children not given this firm and loving parenting will not be equipped with the strength, maturity, and the trust in humankind to emancipate successfully. They will "camp outside the gates" of paradise longing for lost innocence and unable to pick up and engage their humanity.

The One-Minute Scolding

Chapter 7

Love Is Not Enough

The One-Minute Scolding was first conceived as a result of our efforts to help troubled adopted and foster children develop a bond or attachment to their parents. Because all these children had lost several sets of parents prior to their current placement, they had become unwilling or unable to believe and trust that their new parents would not also abandon them. That intense, trusting relationship that is characteristic of the normal attachment between parent and child seemed to be an impossibility to them.

In search of some clues as to how we might break this impasse, we turned to the literature on bonding, which is grounded in observation and analysis of the parent/child relationship. Animal behaviorists, such as Konrad Lorenz and Desmond Morris, have provided us with much useful information about bonding.

How Bonding Begins

As almost everyone knows, baby mammals need milk to survive and only the mother can provide that milk. Should the mother forget her baby and wander off, the baby could die. Baby mammals are also relatively helpless and fall easy prey to predators if they are not protected by a parent. To guarantee the infant's survival, nature seems to have developed a set of behaviors for both infant and mother that fosters an intense attachment to form. This bond compels the mother to return to her baby, to feed it, and to protect it. The bond also directs that baby mammal to stay close to its mother when hungry, frightened, or ill. That is why it is not recommended that humans get too close to a bear cub in the forest. The mother bear will soon arrive, programmed to do all in her rather extensive power to save that cub.

Human infants require many years of protection and care if they are to survive and grow up, so the process of bonding between human parent and child is especially important. This bond does not come about automatically. We find many parents and children for whom this is a difficult process, and a good, strong attachment is not achieved. Sometimes the process has been interrupted by hospitalizations or other separations, or losses of shorter or longer duration. Where the bonding process has been filled with great difficulty, parents and children are conflicted and confused in their feelings towards each other. Almost invariably, those children develop serious problems and become deeply disturbed.

By relying on observation alone, we can readily verify the existence of an intense parent/child bond among most mammals and the destructive consequences of the absence of this bond. Of critical importance, however, is the additional question that behavioral scientists have not yet fully answered: How does this bond normally come into being, and how can it be developed in troubled older children who failed to form such an attachment at the usual time during infancy and childhood?

Let's look at the bonding process in action. For being such a small, helpless creature, a baby is capable of causing powerful feeling in its parents. When a baby is wet and hungry, he can cry in a way that elicits a fairly prompt response. The response is prompt because that cry can cause the mother considerable tension and discomfort. By the time the baby's cry has reached a certain pitch, the mother will put aside her other concerns to hurry off and change the howling baby's diaper. She clucks and croons to him as she quickly cleans him up. Then she finds her comfortable chair, settles in with the child, and begins to feed or nurse him. Most of the time, both mother and child immediately begin to relax. The baby nestles into the curve of the mother's arm in a cozy and comfortable way. He sucks away happily and looks up at his mother. The mother looks back and they smile and coo to each other.

Studies by attachment theorist Bowlby and others have shown that maternal/infant attachment progresses extremely rapidly in the first few hours and days of an infant's life. In addition, they have found that touching, eye contact, crying, and physical interactions between the mother and the baby play vital roles in the development of this attachment. From these and other studies, as well as our observation of parents and children struggling to form satisfying attachments, we have concluded that it is those interactions between infant and parent (speaking, feeding, cooing, smiling, laughing, holding, touching) while going from a state of high excitation to a state of relaxation, which actually form the bond and then cause that bond to grow and to strengthen between the infant and the parent.

"Peek-a-boo" is a game mothers often play quite naturally with their babies. The game strengthens their bond. It is also an excellent demonstration of bonding in action.

The mother hides her face behind her hands. The baby cannot see her and responds with agitation and then anxiety. "Mother has disappeared!" "Boo!" She whips her hands away from her face. "Mama has returned!" The baby is flooded with relief and delight. Over and over they repeat the game. It is an emotional roller coaster for the baby. Mama is gone: Anxiety! Mama returns: Delicious relief and joy! These games and variations of them are repeated day after day. Playfully, intuitively, the mother has created a ritual that strengthens their attachment. Such games prepare the child for those real-life situations when the mother must be out of sight for longer periods. The short burst sessions of peek-a-boo have taught the child that he might lose sight of his mother for awhile and that, while this may cause him anxiety, she will always return. In this way, the child builds up trust.

Again, it is the process of reaching high emotion in both the mother and the child, then coming down to a relaxed state, that is the essence of bonding.

Because it is usually the mother who has the opportunity to play these bonding games and bring relief when the child is distressed, the mother/child bond tends to be the strongest. However, this process works for anyone who has such an interaction with the child: father, grandparent, or sibling.

The leading exponent of attachment theory, John Bowlby, has emphasized in his series of books on attachment and loss that "there is a propensity in human beings to form strong, affectionate bonds to significant others." He has explained that many forms of emotional distress and personality disorders in children are the consequence of separation and loss of a parent. The most intense emotions arise during the formation, maintenance, disruption, and renewal of attachment relationships. The threat of losing the parent arouses *anxiety* in the child, whereas actual loss gives rise to *sorrow*. Both the threat of loss and actual loss are likely to arouse *anger*.

Our Own Research

Over an 18-month period we studied 26 children who had been taken from their natural parents because of neglect or abuse. Each had experienced multiple placements in adoptive or foster homes by the time we saw them. Each was referred for psychiatric evaluation or treatment because of pervasive maladaptive behaviors and attitudes. We found that (1) none of the children had developed a satisfactory bond to their current parents; (2) some of them were able, even compelled, to evoke strong feelings in their parents by annoying or dangerous misbehavior, which resulted in strong feelings, to be sure, but feelings that were also negative.

Their parents had all tried a variety of disciplinary measures and punishments to stop the negative behaviors in children—spankings, rewards, restrictions—and though the punishments were frequently consistent and often harsh, they didn't get the more adaptive behaviors they had hoped for. Even though abandonment was what they feared most, these children risked behaving as though they expected—or even wanted—their parents to abandon them, just as the others before them had done.

Could it be that these children's antisocial and annoying behaviors, which constantly provoked high emotions in their parents, were some clumsy but elemental compulsion to initiate the first stage of bonding? If so, the adoptive parents were missing their cues. All of the parents revealed that eventually they resorted to one common form of response. In their annoyance and desperation, they banished the children from their proximity. "Go to your room!" or "I've had enough, I'm going out!" At the point of highly aroused feelings in both the parent and the child, the child was abandoned or distanced and the process was interrupted only to repeat itself like a needle stuck on a record. The children had achieved their feared goal: abandonment. When the family finally came for psychiatric help, the parents commonly admitted defeat and felt that someone else should take over the task of raising their difficult youngster. The parents felt angry and frustrated. Love and the best of intentions had not been enough, and there were no rewards. They felt like failures as parents. The children in turn sensed the imminent and feared response to their actions: another rejection and abandonment. Their actions were again self-defeating, their fears, self-fulfilling.

With the help of Bowlby's studies on attachment and bonding, we discovered a clue which resolved this vicious circle: children in danger or distress seek out and need the proximity of their parents to feel safe. Parents protect and are a source of gratification. While the child, in his own primitive manner, was seeking out all and any behavior necessary to arouse the intense feelings that launched or strengthened attachment, our parents were aborting the next step necessary: proximity. Unable to read the obscure meaning of the child's behavior, they were actually doing the opposite of what was necessary by banishing the youngster from their sight. Thus, a bond was not formed, and the attachment was not strengthened.

The One-Minute Scolding

The bond itself became our "patient." Now the parents had to be taught to continue the bonding process to the end in order to make attachment possible. We instructed the parents not to punish their children with banishment or withdrawal. Instead, they were told that when the child misbehaved to take the child on their laps, and to scold him or her vigorously and with feeling. By the time the child had been aroused to an emotional response (sad look, tears, a bowed head), both parent and child would be in a state of strong feeling. The parents then were to change their tone abruptly and become warm and loving. They were to reassure the child of the permanence of their relationship and to tell the child of their real care and concern for him.

In this ritualized "bonding exercise," we taught the parents to display intensely negative and then intensely positive emotions (anger/rage vs. caring/affection) in the interaction, because the wall of defenses that the child had learned to hide behind needed to be penetrated. The defensive wall "kept the parents out" so that the child could remain untouched. The parent had to break through with an expression of strong feeling.

Because it's easy for a parent to prolong the scolding segment of the process, a time limit was set so that the parent would change abruptly from intense negative feeling (lasting no longer than thirty seconds) to intense positive feeling (also thirty seconds) before the child had time to rebuild his defensive walls. Hence, we called the technique the "One-Minute Scolding." This way he would still be open to warmth and love.

At first, the parents found it hard to believe that this simple exercise was going to change their child's behavior. Their dramatic punishments had gotten them nowhere, to be sure. But a reinterpretation of their children's behavior as a clumsy attempt to get their attachment needs met began to make sense to them.

With strong support from a parents' group and their therapists, all of the parents made brave efforts at home. To their surprise, significant changes in their children became apparent almost right away. Although there were failures and regressions, we discovered that whenever parents were able to use the One-Minute Scolding consistently, not only did children misbehave less, but the tone of the parent/child relationship improved dramatically as well. Where once the child's needfulness was manifested by clinging, whining, and attention-seeking behaviors, the parents now reported the child to be more direct, affectionate, and playful. Slowly, they began to see the child developing a conscience. Care and consideration began to replace the atmosphere of warring camps.

What Makes It Work Best?

As we began teaching more parents and other professionals interested in using our technique, we looked for additional theoretical understanding to improve and refine the effectiveness of this new bonding strategy. We also wanted to understand better just why the One-Minute Scolding was an effective discipline in changing behavior. We discovered that there are several important elements which reinforce the technique's effectiveness.

Consistency and Repetition

Important elements in learning are consistency and repetition. Parents who became consistent in their response to a child's misbehavior were rewarded by the child's ability to learn new and more appropriate behaviors. During this learning process, children learn unevenly, and sometimes they seem to resist the teaching process. Effective teachers and parents seem to understand this, and they know that children do not learn a lesson once and for all. They anticipate forgetfulness and even though it may be boring or irksome at times, they are consistent and willing to repeat the right answer or the correct behavior over and over again.

The Right Strength of Feeling

It is important that the forcefulness of the parent not be exaggerated because the child will then focus on his fear of the parent rather than the scolding. Children are afraid of parents with hot tempers, particularly fathers full of rage. Fear tends to preoccupy children with their need for safety, and it becomes impossible for them to attend to the lesson.

Privacy and Distraction

If a laughing or teasing sibling stands on the sidelines, that will distract the child and interrupt the learning process. The One-Minute Scolding is best given in privacy, whenever possible, where one can have the child's undivided attention. One might view the One-Minute Scolding as a teacher-student interaction within which the child's attention is focused on a particular rule that is to be learned. As every teacher knows, privacy or freedom from distraction is essential to giving and receiving a clear message in the shortest length of time.

Clarity

With the right degree of feeling and in a nondistracting environment, the Scolding must now be delivered with utmost clarity. Distinctly and repeatedly the child is given the Scolding: "We don't hit people in this house. I don't want you to hit your sister. Hitting is ugly behavior, and I get very angry with you when you hit your sister."

The Right Length of Time

A parent cannot drone on and on with the Scolding because children learn to "tune out." Once the child is no longer paying attention to the parent, learning stops. The child's attention drifts off, and the message is unheard. A "tuned out" parent also loses interest in teaching.

Reward

Children learn best when they are rewarded for desired behavior. First, the children listen to the scolding part of the One-Minute Scolding, and then we reward them for listening in the second half. The abrupt switch from a high-intensity scolding to a tone of reassurance and affection brings pleasant relief for the child, but it is also rather confusing and disorienting. The child feels as though his emotional and psychological mindset must turn an about-face; now he must focus in an entirely new and different direction. The affectionate words carry the message to him again, and the child hears the lesson even more clearly.

"You know, I think you're such a nifty and special fellow. When you play happily with your sister and when you're having a good time, it makes me happy. I like being your mama, and I want to be the very best mama possible. No matter how naughty you are sometimes, I'll never leave you. Instead, I'll help you. Every time you hit, I'll scold you until you can remember that hitting is not allowed. I'll do that because I love you so much."

The child likes his parents to talk to him in this way. That warm approval of who he is, that assurance of love, rewards him for listening and paying attention to the lesson presented in the first half of the Scolding. The child feels good when praised and treated like this.

Chapter 8

The One-Minute Scolding

How do I apply the One-Minute Scolding? What are the steps involved? How do I get started? Answers to these questions and more are given in this chapter including a specific description of the One-Minute Scolding, as well as examples.

Before we begin, we need to recognize that the One-Minute Scolding is not a punishment that inflicts physical or mental discomfort as a penalty for some offense. Punishment is not good discipline because it causes fear and anxiety in the child that actually *inhibits* learning. The One-Minute Scolding works because as effective discipline, it teaches.

Immediately before a One-Minute Scolding begins, the parent should assess the amount of anger that he or she has inside. Many adults carry a reservoir of negative feelings associated with their employment, disagreements with friends and relatives, and other circumstances. Prior to the One-Minute Scolding the person doing the disciplining must identify and separate the anger they have about other events from the anger over the child's misbehavior. This very short assessment ensures that angry feelings match the misbehavior and not other events of the day. Bringing unrelated anger and other feelings into the disciplining process must be avoided. Following this emotional reality check, the One-Minute Scolding may begin.

Briefly, the *five steps* of a One-Minute Scolding are:

1. Scolding the behavior
2. A moment of transition
3. Positive reaffirmation of the child's worth
4. A short quiz of the rules
5. Affectionate physical contact

Let's look at each of these five steps and get a clearer understanding of their meaning and application.

1. Scolding the Behavior

The first step of the scolding is usually easy to remember, and it's composed of two parts.

First: The parent grasps the child and leads the child to a place separated from other family members and people in general. Distractions will be minimized, and the child will not be embarrassed by being disciplined in front of friends or family.

Second: While the parent touches, holds, or grasps the child, the parent scolds the child for misbehavior when a household rule is broken or a significant order is not obeyed. The parent looks and acts as upset as she feels, but she must be genuine with her feelings and honest with the wording and terminology used in her scolding. The wide spectrum of anger displayed by the parent has many levels of feeling and intensity ranging from mild irritation to fury or rage. We have noted that most fathers must tone their voices down because their anger can come across as excessive, and children become frightened rather than learning the lesson.

Remember that most acts of misbehavior are over trivial things and a great display of anger would be out of proportion to the "crime." Sometimes a kid's misbehavior has life-threatening consequences, and therefore the disciplining process should include a great deal of anger and expression of feeling.

The parent tells the child why she is scolding, explains the rule, and continues until the child responds with signs of feeling: a tear, a sad face, a quivering lip, a downcast look.

In this step, the parent may feel a wide range of feelings, such as annoyance, irritation, anger, fury, rage, frustration, and worry. On the receiving end, the child may be worried, anxious, tense, angry, scared, apprehensive, terrified, tearful, sorry, or remorseful.

The parent should not continue to scold past thirty seconds. (Very young or highly sensitive children require even less scolding time.)

Steps 2, 3, 4, and 5 that follow should take a total of thirty seconds.

2. A Moment of Transition

The transition period that follows the parent's expression of anger and disapproval is very important and must take place in a matter of seconds. The transition is a significant change from angry statements and scolding behavior to warm, loving, emotions and nurturing behavior, and it is a very necessary part of the One-Minute Scolding.

Nobody can *directly* change his or her feelings such as anger and caring. So how do we change our feelings? We first *change our thoughts*, and they must be changed rapidly during the transition to warm, loving thoughts. Then our feelings will "follow" our thoughts, and our feelings will match our new thoughts. Taking a deep breath and moving your muscles while changing your thoughts is also beneficial to the transition. This is how the transition is made within the person doing the disciplining.

Many find it difficult to rapidly develop warm, kind thoughts during the transition period. To help this process, some other time when you are in a calm, neutral mood, develop and memorize a few warm, loving statements about your child. When a transition period occurs again, you will be able to rapidly recall these key phrases from memory, and they will become your thoughts. Warm feelings will follow.

Example: After scolding her child, the mother pauses for a few seconds while changing her angry thoughts to caring ones by reminding herself of how much she loves her son. Her entire attitude is quickly changed. Abruptly, an angry, scolding mother switches to a loving, nurturing mother. Then she is ready to change her disciplining approach and move to Step 3.

3. Positive Reaffirmation of the Child's Worth

Initially, the second half of the scolding is the more difficult to produce. Even though the parent has been somewhat angry, very upset, or maybe even full of rage before the transition in Step 2, he must now reassure the child of his worth. The child needs to know beyond a doubt that he is loved, that he will not be abandoned, that he is capable of changing and learning how to behave, and that he will be helped consistently. The child hears and learns how he'll be able to behave properly. During this step, the child feels the way the parent expresses confidence and tenderness in tone of voice, word content, body language, and touch. The parent is reassuring, warm, and in control.

In this step, the parent reaffirms the child's worth by making a positive verbal statement about him followed by a verbal feeling statement, and this cycle is repeated several times. Positive verbal statements point out good, admirable qualities about the child.

Verbal feeling statements are an expression of warmth, love, and affection by the parent towards the child.

In this step, the parent may feel warm, tender, gentle, caring, hopeful, confident, loving, nurturing, clear, certain, or satisfied. The child may feel surprised, relieved, confused, pleased, remorseful, secure, loved, worthy, or certain.

4. A Short Quiz of the Rules

The parent must check to see if she has effectively taught the rule(s) by giving a short quiz to the child. Questions are to be asked in such a way that the child has to quote the rule that was broken from memory. Ask the child if he understands the rule. When a child says that he doesn't know the rule when quizzed, use that moment as an opportunity to teach the rule again.

If the child's misbehavior could have resulted in painful or significant consequences for himself or someone else, the child should be required explain the possible consequences of breaking the rule in the future (e.g., my sister could fall down; our dog could get hit by a car; I could get burned by a hot pan; I could be suspended from school, etc.).

5. Affectionate Physical Contact

The scolding ends with affectionate physical contact such as a hug for younger children or a warm pat on the back for some older teens. This contact is a symbolic and physical gesture that emphasizes the closeness of the relationship. A hug or pat on the back is primarily a message from the parent that the scolding lesson is ended. By accepting and returning the embrace or physical contact, the child acknowledges the scolding as a loving gesture by the parent.

An Example of a One-Minute Scolding

The Event

Eight-year-old Brad loved to build with his metal erector set, and usually he liked to do it all by himself. He concentrated intently because the set had a battery-powered engine in it, and it was hard to figure out. Brad's five-year-old sister was also in the house, and she had a friend over to play with her. For about thirty minutes the two girls teased Brad, giggled at him, and made a nuisance of themselves. Brad asked the girls to leave him alone, but they wouldn't. Then the girls got right up next to Brad and the table he was working on, and they started moving around pieces of Brad's erector set. That's when Brad exploded. He yelled at the girls and demanded that they get away from him. He punched his sister, and she lost her balance and fell to the floor. Their mother had been in the kitchen and saw much of the outburst of Brad's temper.

The Anger Assessment

Before scolding Brad, the mother did a ten-second inventory or recognition of her anger. She had been rushed all day trying to make several casseroles for a potluck party that night. She was running late and was angry that she had volunteered to do the cooking. She realized that much of her anger was caused by the rush to get things done. She knew that the remaining anger was directed at Brad's misbehavior.

Step 1

The One-Minute Scolding begins. The mother grabbed Brad by the shoulder and led him into the kitchen. Also, she told the girls to stay where they were. Then the mother proceeded to scold Brad.

Mother: "Brad! You hit your sister. We don't hit in this house. It makes me terribly angry when you hurt your sister. I've told you before and you forgot. That's no way for you to get what you want from her. It makes me angry, it hurts her, it solves nothing, and that's just plain naughty behavior."

Brad: (Brad is not to speak in this step, he must listen.)

Step 2

The mother stops scolding and quickly changes her thoughts to warm loving thoughts. She recalls that "he's a good-looking kid, fun to be with, talented, and very smart." Brad is filled with anticipation and waits for his mother's next move.

Step 3

The mother then gives Brad some positive reaffirmation. Her feeling statements follow positive statements.

Mother: "You're such a smart, charming, and talented kid. I am so glad that you're mine.

"I'll help you. I want to be a good mama, so every time you forget and hit your sister, I'll scold you. Soon you'll remember that we don't hit. Even if you forget, I'll just keep reminding you. And never forget that I love you even when you make mistakes.

"You're such a neat brother, and I know that deep down you love your sister. And you know, I love you very much!"

With this positive affirmation, most children feel relieved and reassured of their parents' love.

Step 4

The mother gives Brad a quiz of the rules, and uses this time to teach him proper behavior.

Mother: "Why am I scolding you now?"
Brad: "Because I hit my sister."

Mother: "Right! Good boy!

(She gives him a few praises for knowing what this scolding is about.)

"And why must I scold you every time you make a bad mistake?"
Brad: "Because I'm not supposed to hit my sister."
Mother: "Right! And because I love you so much! What are you supposed to do when you feel mad with your sister?"
Brad: "Come to you for help if I can't handle it."
Mother: "Right."

Step 5

The mother reaches out and gives Brad a hug, and she feels Brad hugging her in return. The scolding is over.

Note: In the previous example, thorough discipline would require the mother to scold Brad's sister for her nagging behavior. Some parents tend to scold one child more than another or make one child guilty for all wrongs when clearly two had some part. When "events" include more than one child, each child should be disciplined separately using the One-Minute Scolding.

Does Anger Usually Last Too Long?

To be angry with your child does not mean that you have stopped loving him. On the contrary, you probably wouldn't feel so angry if you didn't love him so much. Anger is natural and even helpful within certain boundaries.

For parents who are not accustomed to a healthy, appropriate discharge of anger, thirty seconds seems insufficient. Too much unfinished anger is dammed up and ready to explode in an inappropriate way. The One-Minute Scolding offers this parent both a safeguard in its time limit and a vehicle to express strong feelings appropriately. It also helps to terminate an issue that might otherwise have no clear ending.

To experience anger and love as mutually exclusive emotions (feeling one, but not both, at a time) is easy. The parent feels this conflict or seesaw of emotions; one minute there's anger, and in another minute there's love. The child fears the unpredictability of his parent's emotions, and the child doesn't like bad feelings looming over him. All of us have experienced the feeling of being banished to our rooms after having elicited the rage of an exasperated parent. Our bedroom door was a heavy barrier between us and the rest of the family. It seemed as if love had ended, and anger loomed on both sides of the door. Anger and bad feelings lasted too long.

Maurice Sendak, in his famous children's book, *Where the Wild Things Are,* lets us in on the powerful, but charming monsters (thoughts and feelings) that rage and dance in the imagination of Max who was sent to his room by his exasperated mother. Sendak resolves the issue of where mother's love has gone by sending up dinner to Max's room, and the dinner was still warm (meaning Max was forgiven by his mother and her warmth was still there.) The fuzzy cloud of anger was removed by the mother's gesture, and peace was restored in the home. Anger need not last indefinitely!

Almost every child's fear and anger gets tamed eventually, but there are some kids who never master these emotions effectively. Not every child is redeemed soon enough with an honest expression of love. For every child, the One-Minute Scolding has the potential to put anger in its proper place and time if the parent carries it out correctly. The child's much needed love and closeness can be restored.

Are Love and Anger Mutually Exclusive?

The Other Side of the Defense Barrier

The abrupt transition from being angry and upset to being warm and reassuring is a particularly important facet of the One-Minute Scolding. Parents may find that it feels somewhat uncomfortable or contrived at first, especially if they have a large backlog of undischarged anger left over from other frustrations. They may find the balance difficult to create between anger and love. They have to be convinced themselves that anger does not cancel out love. But practice and the formula of the One-Minute Scolding itself will help the parent strike a more natural balance in time.

The abrupt switch of feelings is particularly important for the well-defended child. Such a child has learned to keep his parent "out," and he refuses to let his parents' feelings and actions touch him in any significant way. Children who develop this defense to an extreme are likely to develop sociopathic ways of dealing with life's problems. These are the children who have difficulty developing a conscience that works. The abrupt change of feelings from anger to love in the One-Minute Scolding is an effective way for parents to catch such a defensive youngster off guard and touch him suddenly with positive feelings. This reverses the development of a defensive and antisocial lifestyle.

The use of the One-Minute Scolding gives the parents a framework in which to deal with their own feelings appropriately. An explosive, destructive father or a nagging, complaining mother can be transformed into a parent who expresses feelings about their child's behavior in a mature and adaptive way. The father doesn't hurl the roller skate against the garage door as before, but now he states clearly, "I get mad as heck when I find your toys scattered all over the driveway where they rust, get lost, or cause accidents." He incorporates his feeling expression into the scolding portion. In so doing, not only is he able to discharge his anger immediately and safely, but he is also able to continue to teach the lesson he wants the child to learn. When a parent uses a mature expression of angry feeling, the child, in turn, learns not only that (1) feeling anger and expressing how you feel is natural and right, but also that (2) there is an appropriate and adaptive way to express those feelings. "If my Dad is angry at me, he tells me. This does not mean that he doesn't love me anymore."

A mature and adaptive expression of anger does not

> *Blame:* "You make me mad!" Rather: "I get awfully mad when...";
>
> *Act out:* such as hurling the roller skate against the garage door and cursing;
>
> *Humiliate the other person:* "You rotten, sniveling kid!"; or finally,
>
> *Muddy the issue directly at hand:* "You let the garbage pile up again, and last week you just left the garden tools outside, and..." Rather: "Each evening after supper, I want you to take out the garbage."

To be angry is natural, and its immediate expression does not have to destroy anyone or anything. Neither does anger mean: "I don't love you anymore."

Many families now use this technique, and we have found that if the parents are able to use it consistently, following the guidelines in Chapter 8, it can replace or augment most other forms of discipline. Some parents find that using "time out" or "natural consequences" can give spice and variety to a parent's discipline. Others believe that most disciplinary measures can be effective if administered in a kind, firm, and consistent way. These forms of discipline send the child away, or leave the child and parent still very upset. Because of this, if used as a sole means of discipline, "time-outs" or spanking can prove ineffective. We've observed that the best results occur in families who either replace their old methods with the One-Minute Scolding, or at least prioritize the scolding over other techniques.

After twenty years of using the One-Minute Scolding we have seen the following effects:

* It changes the child's behavior, teaching him to choose those behaviors that reward him with a satisfying state of affairs for himself and for those around him.
* It teaches the child that his behaviors have consequences.
* It teaches the value of working through a problem with communication.
* It gives both parent and child a model for the adaptive expression of feelings.
* It forms and/or strengthens the bond between parent and child, and it teaches trust.
* In teaching trust, it enables the child to develop a conscience.
* It is a technique that is useful for any family.

All too often disapproving looks, the "silent treatment," or banishment from the scene make a child feel rejected and abandoned at precisely the moment he needs to know that his parents are loving and strong enough to help him when he causes trouble. The fear he now feels blocks his ability to learn the nature of his misbehavior or how he is to change it. The child is left only with feelings of fear, anger, and sadness. Anger rules the home, and love is far away.

Fortunately, the One-Minute Scolding offers a new concept of discipline that transforms both the parent-child relationship and the very nature of the parent's disciplining techniques. In most cases where children are disciplined, anger lasts too long while love is unexpressed. Although the feeling states of anger and love cannot exist at the same instant in time, anger and love are counterbalanced during the One-Minute Scolding. Anger is expressed during the first half of a minute, and love is in the second half. This has the effect of condensing and merging anger and love within a minute of time, and for practical purposes, they aren't mutually exclusive anymore. Anger and love are confined to and balanced by the sixty-second period. The dual expression of anger and love is the most important and revolutionary concept of the One-Minute Scolding.

Difficult and unnatural as this close combination of opposite emotions strikes us, it is the identical pattern found in the ways infants and parents bond. Both parent and child progress from feelings of high excitation descending to relaxation producing bonding or attachment between the two. It is the ability of the One-Minute Scolding to synthesize this pattern with the same sliding range of two strong feelings that accounts for its remarkable success as a disciplinary approach. By taking advantage of the high feeling states (anger and love) in the parents' reactions to misconduct and ending in a calm and comfortable state of relaxation, the One-Minute Scolding helps parent and child bond, creating a closer attachment.

How Do I Apply the One-Minute Scolding?

Like any good tool, the One-Minute Scolding has to be used properly for it to work well. Even though the Scolding should never take more than a minute, it has to be administered with all of its parts and in the right order and manner. You shouldn't use it unless you're clear about what to do and how to do it. A part of the Scolding is worse than none at all.

Although the One-Minute Scolding is simple in structure, it is sophisticated in nature. The underlying feeling patterns and their order and progression are the roots of success for the One-Minute Scolding. But it is not necessary to understand its sophisticated nature to apply the method or for it to work. It is necessary, however, to administer it *correctly* and *consistently*. In Chapter 7 we explained how the technique of the One-Minute Scolding was developed and improved over the last 20 years, but you need not have read that chapter to use the One-Minute Scolding. Some parents, however, will appreciate the process of how we put the approach together; understanding its principles will encourage them in their efforts. Furthermore, parents will see that its basic principles are applicable to many other interpersonal relationships.

Does It Really Work in Only a Minute?

The One-Minute Scolding has a surprisingly simple structure and takes one minute of your time to administer, so it isn't time consuming. But within that simple structure, a powerful range of feelings is to be expressed and compressed.

We all know that a minute is sixty seconds or one-sixtieth of an hour, but how do we know how long a minute is while giving a One-Minute Scolding? We have a feel for one minute of time, and that is what we go by. After a One-Minute Scolding we must ask whether it was too short or too long. Next time, we make adjustments in the time length, and our goal is always to keep the scolding to a minute, not less, not more.

In the past when we disciplined a child for a misbehavior, often we felt we weren't clear or effective unless we maintained a stance of disapproval over a long period of time—hours, or even days! Some parents felt that a child needed to remain uncomfortable for a long time to learn his or her lesson. But we know now that children learn quickly, and we know that to remain disapproving of a child for a long time only diminishes that child's sense of his basic good nature. Feeling diminished interferes with the child's development as well as his capacity to behave well and to succeed.

How Do I Get Started?

The parent, as a mature adult, is strong enough to learn and undertake what may initially be uncomfortable. But after the initial discomfort, it will begin to feel more natural. The ability to experience conflicting emotions while maintaining one's composure and sense of balance is the essence of maturity. This ability is not a natural instinct; it must be developed.

Parents need support and encouragement in implementing the One-Minute Scolding technique at first. Old habits of discipline are not easy to change, and when one tries to form a new habit it is easy to give up at the first hint of difficulty or resistance.

Parents, struggling to learn and apply this technique, deal with their own conflicting feelings and discover a new strength within themselves. This strength carries over to a variety of interpersonal relationships, not just the parent-child bond. The child learns with the parents how to express strong, even conflicting feelings honestly and appropriately.

Before putting the One-Minute Scolding into practice for the first time, we encourage parents to do the following: (1) Read this book and think the method through; (2) practice the method with your spouse or a friend until you master it; (3) realize that you will make mistakes and that you aren't going to give a perfect One-Minute Scolding; (4) practice and critique your scolding method (your ability to do the five steps adequately within a minute); and (5) applaud yourself for the effort you make with each practice. Afterwards, numbers (3), (4), and (5) should be done regularly while actually using the One-Minute Scolding.Later in the book we address in detail the specific problems and difficulties that both parents and children encounter initially with this technique. Parents often face clever defenses by their children to the One-Minute Scolding, and these parents will find help and insight in Chapter 11.

When Will I See Results?

Some children whose problems are not severe learn quickly and respond within days with improved behavior and better feelings about themselves and their parents. Most children require a few weeks of consistent scolding before they respond positively. A few extremely difficult children require several months. But as long as you stay with the technique, you will eventually achieve your goal of improving your child's behavior while strengthening your own sense of joy and happiness within your family.

At this point, however, it is enough for you to know that administering the One-Minute Scolding is, in fact, easy. The difficulty comes in delivering the scolding consistently and maturely, even when it doesn't seem to be working right away. We can assure you that your hard work in sticking with this technique will be richly rewarded.

Again, What Are Those Five Steps?

The One-Minute Scolding provides a simple structure for the parent to discipline his or her child. The method is really not all scolding and has five parts that must follow a brief anger assessment:

1. Scolding the behavior
2. A moment of transition
3. Positive reaffirmation of the child's worth
4. A short quiz of the rules
5. Affectionate physical contact

Chapter 9

From 18 Months to 18 Years

This chapter is not meant to be a cookbook on discipline. The examples used are rather general. Because real-life children, parents, and situations vary greatly in their idiosyncrasies and possibilities, your personal expression while disciplining a child is not likely to match these examples exactly.

It is important for parents to remember that the One-Minute Scolding can be started and applied at any point in the development of a child as a disciplinary procedure. In other words, just because your youngster is already 14, it is not too late to have a real impact on his behavior and effect a change.

An important point in this chapter is that the general *form* of the One-Minute Scolding remains the same, but the *tone* and *intensity* varies with:

* the age of the child
* the temperament of the child
* the severity of the misdeed

That's a No-No

At 18 months, Stephanie is bright and inquisitive, and the TV buttons fascinate her. Although it is not dangerous to play with the buttons, her parents are annoyed when they have to readjust the set each time they want to watch the news. So they have made a rule that is important to them. Most everything that is dangerous to the baby has already been removed, locked up, or in some way baby-proofed. Not playing with buttons is one of the few rules that they wish to teach Stephanie. Stephanie knows this.

One morning, Stephanie toddles up to the television set and begins to play with the buttons. Her mother can tell that Stephanie knows this may be forbidden because she looks expectantly at her mother as she fiddles with the controls.

The mother quietly says, "No." Stephanie looks at her mother but continues to play with the buttons.

Her mother repeats, "Stephanie, no. Go away from the television set!" Stephanie's eyes widen. She watches her mother very carefully but does not leave the set. She keeps her fingers on the dial. Stephanie is disobeying her mama.

If a child does not learn to obey her parents, she frequently misunderstands her power, controls the family, and becomes "the boss." A family "bossed" by a small child is a family in considerable distress. So her mother uses the One-Minute Scolding. But because Stephanie is very young, the Scolding half must be short, and the feelings expressed should not be so intense as to overwhelm her.

Stephanie's mother approaches and says firmly: "No! No! You may not play with the television set, Stephanie."

When the mother says "No," she may shake her finger or frown at Stephanie to communicate her disapproval visually. The voice and gestures are forceful enough, so Stephanie will feel a little frightened. The mother sees Stephanie become a bit tearful and her lower lip trembles. Perhaps she drops her head and her body sags. That marks the end of the first half on the One-Minute Scolding. It may not have lasted ten seconds.

The mother then picks Stephanie up, holds her closely and warmly and says, "Stephanie, I love you. You are a sweet child. I don't want you to play with the TV. That is a no-no. Mama loves you, but Mama does not want you to play with the TV." As Stephanie quiets down, her mother turns and points to the television saying gently, "Stephanie, that's a No. The television is a No. I do not want you to play with it." Stephanie's mother takes her from the television and interests her in something else.

Stephanie is alert and responsive, but one act of discipline by her mother or father may not be enough to establish that fiddling with the television is forbidden. Most likely, Stephanie will try to play with the buttons again. Later, Stephanie's father sees that she is playing with it again. For the sake of consistency and balance, both parents should be equally prepared to discipline their children when they break a rule. Furthermore, one parent should not be perceived as the one who administers a majority of the One-Minute Scoldings. Stephanie's parents have agreed that they both will help her with this rule. As Stephanie looks uncertainly at her father, she reaches out and plays with one of the buttons. Immediately her father goes up and, in a stern voice and manner, says, "No! The television set is a No."

Stephanie drops to the floor, wailing as though she had been spanked. The first half of the Scolding is over. Her father picks her up and comforts her. As soon as she can respond to him, he directs her gaze towards the television and says, "The TV is a No, you may not play with the TV set." He is warm and comforting. "I love you, Stephanie, you are a good little girl. I know you can learn not to play with the TV."

Then, he too takes Stephanie to another place where she will not be tempted to play with the television again.

This scenario may need to be repeated several times. Each episode takes no more than ten to fifteen seconds. The child will learn very quickly not to play with the TV set.

There is no need to spank fingers, nor is it wise to put the TV set out of reach. Most children can learn quickly to leave things alone if they are consistently and effectively disciplined to do so.

The Explorer

Now we apply the One-Minute Scolding to a four-year-old who likes to explore and visit the neighbors. Little David has been playing quietly in the garage with the door open. His mother knows there is nothing in the garage that he could get into that could hurt him, so she is in the garden planting.

At some point, his mother becomes aware that David is no longer nearby. She finds him in the neighbor's garage with his four-year-old friend, Troy. They are playing "gas station" and are filling the gas tank of the automobile with water from the garden hose. David's mother recognizes the extreme danger immediately. They have flushed out gasoline, and it has spilled onto the garage floor. If ignited, the gasoline would envelop both boys and the entire garage in flames.

She grabs both boys, literally dragging them out of danger. She alerts Troy's parents, and calls the fire department. Only after ten minutes of frantic activity does she turn her attention to David.

David and Troy are fascinated by all the activity, especially by the fire engines. They had already forgotten that they were responsible for all this excitement. So when David's mother gets around to disciplining David, he is unprepared for her anger. Kneeling so that she is face-to-face with David, she holds him firmly by both shoulders. She knows that she must teach him *never* to play that game again. She may not have a second chance.

"David, you've made a terrible mistake! I am very upset with you! Playing with gasoline is *dangerous*! I don't want you ever to do that again. You could have started a fire and burned yourself terribly. You must *never, never* play with gasoline again."

There is no doubt that David's mother is extremely upset. He can feel the agitation in her voice, in the hold that she has on his shoulders, and in her body posture and language. Small children are very responsive to strong feelings in their parents, and David is no exception. He responds by crying.

His mother folds him into her arms. Perhaps she weeps with him, discharging her anxiety. Through her tears she tells David, "David, I love you so much. If anything ever happened to you, I would be so upset. You are a wonderful boy, but you must be careful. You must never play with gasoline again. I want to be such a good mama. I have to teach you not to do things like that. You must not do dangerous things like that. I love you so much that I am going to discipline you every time you make a mistake."

David stops his crying. He is aware that his mother is no longer angry but is earnest and intense. Now she makes David look at her directly. She asks, "David, why am I upset with you?"

David replies, "I played gas station with gasoline."

"Are you ever going to do that again?"

"No, Mama," says David.

"David, tell me, 'Mama, I won't play with gasoline again.'"

David responds, "Mama, I won't play with gasoline again."

David's mother takes him by the hand and together they return home. The Scolding is over. We hope David will never need another lesson about the dangers of gasoline.

Parents must teach children to avoid what is dangerous. It is their responsibility to protect them from danger, as well as to teach them how to avoid those dangers themselves. A child quickly learns that some mistakes are more serious than others if the parent's emotional response varies. When children put themselves in truly dangerous situations, parents must respond with strong, vigorous feelings in contrast to mild disappointment at the child's difficulty in learning table manners or other skills that are not so vital. In very serious matters, children need to learn their lesson the first time. There may be no second chance.

A Strong Parent Can Be Trusted to Handle Monsters

Brittany is six. She has been having nightmares and waking up two or three times a night. She cries and refuses to be consoled unless one of her parents stays in her room or she is allowed to sleep with them in their bed. The nightmares began the day Brittany's mother was delayed for half an hour, and Brittany had to wait at school. She had cried and was afraid she was forgotten. Although the incident had not been her fault, Brittany's mother felt guilty. She felt she should have been there on time so that Brittany would not have been so frightened. It was, therefore, easy for Brittany to manipulate her mother into allowing her to sleep in mother and father's bed.

After a telephone consultation with Brittany's pediatrician, her parents decided to make Brittany stay in her own bed, even if she is frightened. The next time Brittany appears at her parents' bedroom door looking forlorn and frightened, her mother responds in a firm voice and says, "Brittany, go back to bed."

Brittany begins to cry and says, "But I'm scared. There's a monster in my closet." Brittany's mother gets up, takes Brittany back to her room and says, "Well, let's see." They both go to the closet and look. Brittany's mother does not try to prove that there are no monsters, by turning on the lights, etc. She wisely realizes that the "monsters" of Brittany's fantasies are as real to Brittany and just as frightening as any visible monster might be. Those things that go "bump in the night" are the unexpressed angers and fears of her daytime experiences.

But for now the lesson Brittany must learn is twofold. She is to ask for help when she needs comfort. She will not have to handle such strong feelings by herself. But she is also to remain in her own bed. Mother, not Brittany, is in control. The monster has apparently fled. Then mother tucks Brittany into her own bed, gives her a hug and says, "Brittany, I know you are scared. But Mommy and Daddy are here and all you have to do is call me and I'll help you. If any monster scares you, I can deal with him easily. Now, you go to sleep. If you wake up afraid, you may call me for help. But stay in your bed."

Brittany is not happy. She was afraid of that monster in her closet. Furthermore, she does not trust that her mother or father will protect her. After all, she was forgotten at school. She tries to sleep, but her fear returns and becomes greater and greater. Finally, she gets up and dashes to her mother and father's bed and tries to climb in between them because it's such a warm and safe place.

Her mother wakes up. Quietly, but firmly, she takes Brittany back to her own room. She sits down on Brittany's bed, and puts Brittany on her lap.

"Brittany, I am angry with you. I know you are afraid that there may be another monster in your closet. I am angry with you because you don't trust me. You don't think that I know how to take care of that monster. I can. If you call me I'll come in and help you. But you disobeyed me and got out of bed again. I am disciplining you because you didn't call me. You disobeyed me and got into my bed. That bed is for Daddy and me. Your bed is for you. You may not sleep with me in my bed. I get very angry with you when you do not obey me. If you are worried or frightened, just call Daddy or me and one of us will come. I am very angry with you, Brittany."

The mother continues until she knows Brittany has begun to learn her lesson. Brittany weeps. He mother changes her way of holding Brittany and is soft and accepting. "You are a sweet girl. I know you are afraid. I will protect you, and I will take care of you. That's the job of Mommies and Daddies. I love you so much that I have to discipline you when you don't obey. I'm going to discipline you every time you make a mistake like that because I love you. I want to be such a good mommy for you. I want you to grow up to be a big strong girl. You must trust me and you must obey me.

"Don't worry, I'll help you. Every time you forget and don't trust me, I'll discipline you. Soon you will understand that you must call me when you're worried or scared."

Her mother then begins the next part of the Scolding and asks,

"Brittany, why am I disciplining you?"

"Because I climbed into your bed. Instead I should call you."

"Yes, Brittany. Every time you make a mistake like that, I'm going to discipline you because I love you and I want to be a good mommy for you. Do you understand?"

Brittany nods. Her mother gives her a warm hug, helps Brittany back into bed, tucks her in and goes back to her own bedroom. If Brittany again forgets and crawls into bed with her parents she will have another Scolding until she knows that Mother or Father will not relent and allow her to sleep in their bed. But her parents will insist that Brittany ask them to help her with her fear.

Brittany's anger and fear of being abandoned arose out of the incident when she was not picked up in time from school. Sometimes those things happen. But when parents are strong, consistent, and warm, they prove they can be trusted not to abandon a child. Furthermore, a strong parent can be trusted to handle closet monsters easily.

Late for Dinner, Again

Peter is 10. He practices soccer just about every afternoon and has been coming home late for dinner despite instruction from his parents that he is to be home by five thirty.

His family is well into dinner when he arrives home happy and flushed. He is at least forty-five minutes late. Obviously, he has lost track of the time again.

Peter's father gets up and says, "Peter, let's go into your bedroom. I have to discipline you."

Peter's face falls. He follows his father into the bedroom and tries to explain why he was delayed.

"No excuses, Peter. You have a watch, and you know we expect you home by five thirty." The father doesn't let Peter argue. He sternly holds Peter's shoulder, looks at him, and "scolds."

"Peter, I am very angry with you. You were supposed to be home at five thirty, and it is now six twenty. You are late and I am angry with you. I am really upset, Peter. And we all get worried. We have warned you repeatedly, and you seem not to hear us. You know the rule that we eat our meals all together. There is no excuse for you not to be here on time. Your soccer practice is over at a quarter to five and we have allowed you plenty of time to josh around with your friends and still be home by five thirty. Yesterday, you told me that you understood, you told us all that you would be home by five thirty at the latest. You forgot again. I really am furious with you, Peter."

Peter is shaken. He had forgotten. He remembers clearly that his parents had warned him that he must be home by five thirty. For some reason, he just did not remember. He had enjoyed the soccer and playing with his friends. He had enjoyed talking with them and fooling around with his bike after practice, and he had truly forgotten his promise to be home at five thirty. He feels terrible. His father gets mad as heck with him and when that happens, it's scary to look at his father.

The father sees that Peter is sad and a little frightened. His grip on Peter's shoulder softens. His tone of voice softens.

"Peter, I love you a lot. You are a fine son. I care heaps about you. In fact, I'm disciplining you because I love you, and because I care about you. Especially, I want to be a good father to you. I'm disciplining you because you made a thoughtless mistake. You promised you'd be home by five thirty so that we could eat our evening meal together. I know you forgot and didn't do it on purpose. But I surely hope that this scolding will help you remember tomorrow night. Because, if you forget again, I'm going to discipline you again. I won't forget.

"In fact, it's easy for me to discipline you, Peter, because that is what a loving dad does for his kids. Every time you make a mistake like this, every time you forget and don't obey, I'll discipline you. That's just to help you. It's no big deal, Peter. O.K.?"

Peter nods. His head is lowered and he looks subdued. "Why will I discipline you? What are you to remember?" His father asks him quickly for the lesson learned, and Peter repeats the message.

His father gives him a warm hug and says, "O.K., Peter, let's go eat dinner, and we won't talk any more about it."

"O.K., Dad, I'll remember next time."

We all forget, and Peter is no exception. So there is no need to make Peter stop playing soccer, or to humiliate him, or spank him, or isolate him from the rest of the family. Peter's parents are happy that he plays soccer and has his friends. But of course they also want him to learn to obey and respond to their wishes. They feel strongly about the importance of mealtimes as family times, as a pleasant opportunity to share stories and re-establish ties. Soccer and family dinners do not have to cancel each other out.

If Peter forgets again, his parents' feelings will increase in intensity and should be expressed in the One-Minute Scolding. Before long, Peter will remember to be home for dinner.

Pot Is Forbidden

Fourteen-year-old Allison has never been a problem. She does well in school, has friends, and generally is a thoughtful child in her family. So, her mother is surprised and upset when, one day, Allison comes home from school with red eyes and cheeks flushed, looking very guilty, and smelling of marijuana. Allison has given in to peer pressure or to her curiosity about pot. At her school, pot is used by many of her peers.

Her parents have often discussed with the children their concerns about marijuana, tobacco, alcohol, and other drugs. Allison always agreed with their principles. She seemed to understand and agree with their explanation of why drugs must be avoided. So this mother is amazed and shocked that Allison could do something so "out of character."

As a good parent, Allison's mother deals with the problem immediately and honestly. She will not postpone the issue until her husband gets back, and though such a disturbing problem has not come up with her other children, she is determined to engage it immediately.

She says, "Allison, come with me to the den." Her voice is stern and intense. Allison knows she is in trouble. She goes off with her mother and stands with her head hung down and shoulders slumped forward. "Allison, you have been smoking marijuana. I am terribly angry with you. We have been very clear with you, both your father and I, about the use of such drugs. Marijuana can be harmful. It is illegal and utterly forbidden. We don't want you to put harmful substances in your body. Actually, Allison, I am completely surprised at you. I really cannot believe that you gave in to some of those kids and smoked marijuana. I figured you were strong enough to withstand that kind of group thinking. There are countless other ways to share friendships without jeopardizing your health and safety. Pot is a dumb cop-out, Allison, as far as I'm concerned. If life feels difficult for kids at 14, it's for parents to be helpful by taking a strong position. Pot would be a stupid way to skip out of the feelings that are common at your age. I am so angry with you."

Her mother's voice is intensely angry and full of disappointment. Allison feels terrible, and she realizes she made a bad mistake. Actually, she knew that her mother and father would be very upset with her if she tried marijuana. Allison starts to cry.

At once her mother stops the angry half of the Scolding. She gathers Allison into her arms and holds her tight. "Allison, I love you so awfully much. I think you are a wonderful person. You hardly ever are a worry to us. Actually, you give us a lot of joy. Your schoolwork is good, you are kind, thoughtful, and responsible. I admire you. At your age, I realize how important it is to be part of the group and that you'd be curious about pot. Kids are just curious about new things. I suppose it doesn't look to you like pot is hurting any of those other kids. But I want you to stay away from it. Your dad and I feel that smoking marijuana is harmful."

She knows Allison is feeling sad and guilty about doing something that was clearly forbidden. She finishes the last half of the Scolding with a hug, saying, "Look Allison, I don't want you to smoke marijuana. I don't want you to smoke tobacco, drink alcohol, or take drugs. You are mistaken if you think those substances can't harm you. Is that clear to you? I want to be a good mom and do a good job. This is all I'm going to say. I don't want you to do it again. If you make a mistake again like that, what can you expect from me? I will discipline you again. You must remember, no matter what, I love you."

Actually, Allison is relieved. Her parents have stood by their values, and it makes her feel safe and secure knowing that they stick up for their values—always have and always will. She does worry what her father will think when he learns that she's tried pot, but she knows that he will not discipline her. She has been disciplined already, and the Scolding is over.

Be Home by Midnight

Michael is 17. He has made a contract with his parents: he may use the family car to go to the football game and dance if he is home by midnight. He has also agreed that if he runs into any problems and expects to be late, he will call. He dashes out, happy about the evening ahead. His parents, however, feel pangs of worry. Michael is bright, sensible, and even thoughtful, but like any teenager, he's occasionally shown lapses in judgment. Sometimes he does very dumb things. This is not because he is indifferent, stupid, or uncaring, but because his judgment is not always mature. He is a good driver, but he tends to show off with his friends and has had to be reminded to drive within the speed limit. His parents know how important it is for teenagers to be able to drive. Besides, there's no way for him to get around this big city without a car. Bus connections are impossible at night. But the thought of his driving the car on the crowded Friday night freeway fills them with anxiety.

Midnight comes and goes. Twelve thirty, one o'clock—both parents are frantic. They can't erase thoughts of squealing brakes, ambulances, flashing lights, hospital emergency rooms. Their anxiety turns into anger.

At one fifteen, just as they consider calling the police, they hear the family car enter the driveway. There he is. Their anxiety transforms into a full-blown rage. Michael opens the door and is met by two furious parents. It's clear enough. He knows he has made a serious mistake.

"Michael, you really blew it. You really made a bad mistake!" Dad grabs him by the shoulder and "scolds" in a loud and agitated voice. He reminds Michael of their agreement. He tells Michael how worried and angry they have been. Michael listens to him and feels guilty and a little sad. He knows he's made a bad mistake. Then his Dad abruptly makes the transition from loud "scolding" to being warm and concerned. Now Michael really feels terrible.

"Michael, your Mom and I love you a lot. We care so much for you. We were terrified that you'd made some error in judgment and had an accident. We want you to use the car, even though we are a bit anxious when you do. We want you to be able to go out and have a good time with your friends. We know you are a sensible and thoughtful driver, but when you are late and don't call, we become worried and angry. Every possible accident races through our minds, and we sit here scared and helpless."

"Look, we are disciplining you because we hate feeling so terrified. You know you can call us to say you'll be late. There is no reason whatsoever why you cannot assure us that you are safe and that there's a reason for being late. We expect you to honor your agreements. You promised us that you would call us if you couldn't be home by midnight."

Michael felt uncomfortable while his parents were "scolding" him, but he could cope with their anger and disappointment. It was when they abruptly became warm and caring and loving to him that he became so extremely uncomfortable that all he wanted to do was escape. He felt ashamed that he did not phone. When they both gave him a brief hug and sent him to bed, he was immensely relieved.

Teenagers are especially uncomfortable with the second half of the One-Minute Scolding. The first half is easier to cope with; it's easier to agree that they were mistaken than it is to be defined as some "great kid." The reason for this is because the teenager feels guilty. Most teenagers learn quickly that to avoid the discomfort of the second half of the Scolding, they have to obey their parents and keep those rules that they know in their hearts are reasonable.

Chapter 10

Discipline During Adolescence

For children and adolescents raised in average situations with average parents, the One-Minute Scolding usually is more than adequate for changing misbehavior. But some kids are more resistant initially because they have experienced particular hindrances such as discipline strategies that don't work, having parents who have more than their share of problems, being raised without much love, being given too little or too many freedoms, and having psychological or emotional problems. For these needy kids, it takes longer for the One-Minute Scolding to do its job. In some needy kids, no change in behavior is seen by using the One-Minute Scolding *alone*. This chapter covers the factors affecting the discipline-learning process, primarily in adolescents where problems abound. Some of these factors are also relevant to children twelve and under.

An adolescent is defined as a young person who is not a child anymore, and is not yet an adult. These youths find themselves in a phase of life that has constant changes physically, emotionally, and socially. With the addition of each new peer comes challenges to the teen's beliefs and values. Almost every week, the teenager looks in the mirror and sees changes, and every week at school he experiences conflicts and challenges. During this transformation to adulthood, a great deal of learning takes place, but not all the lessons of life teach good behavior. Although most teens can display incredible insight, they usually shock us with their lack of judgment. Teenagers with all types of temperaments experience difficulties growing up, and these range from an absence of love, stability, and even a provider of basic needs, to parents who show love, spend time with their teens, and are equipped with discipline techniques that work.

Some adolescents accept guidance readily and see the way through their problems, while others get stuck in them. All of the possible barriers teens may experience need to be discussed in relation to applying the One-Minute Scolding. Then the parent will be aware of the factors that can hinder discipline or the learning process, and he or she can make some corrections. In the rough world in which teenagers live, will caring parents raise them, or by default, will peers, television, and their own physical changes be their only guide?

Sometime in life, most parents are told that "if you haven't taught your children how to behave before they reach their teen years, no more opportunities exist." "A teenager has a mind of his/her own and to try to change it is fruitless." These statements are far from the truth. Each teenager has a will, and it allows him to choose to follow the rules or not. Wills can be redirected. Each teen has erected a set of beliefs about the world, and beliefs can always be changed. Each adolescent has constructed defenses that help him escape pain and strategies that yield pleasure. The biggest fortress can be taken apart one stone at a time, and new channels can be made for the youth's pursuit of pleasure. In short, each teenager is capable of change. With regular One-Minute Scoldings and proper action taken for the influencing factors described in this chapter, a teenager can adopt new behavior. Whether a youth has lived "on the street" for a year or has been spoiled in the lap of luxury and opportunity, no kid is hopeless.

Factors that influence the application of the One-Minute Scolding and strategies for making it more effective follow.

How Do Kids Spell Love?

They spell it, TIME. A young girl sees that someone loves her when "that someone" spends time with her. Many of today's parents have little quality time to spend with their children. Few have the time and energy to participate in an activity with their teenager. This lack of time is often misinterpreted as a lack of love. But is love really love if it isn't expressed? And how can love be expressed if a parent doesn't spend quality time with their child?

Spending time with your kid creates a "bridge" over which your thoughts, values, and feelings can pass. No time means no "bridge." When you give the "affirming half" of the One-Minute Scolding, will your words about love and worth seem shallow because you haven't spent sufficient time with your daughter? If she feels loved, the second half of the One-Minute Scolding will be all the more powerful.

Achieving Balance

Is your teenager living a balanced life? For this to be true, your child's physical, emotional, social, and spiritual areas of life are each given attention, and none of these four areas dominates the teen's life. If one area is neglected, the kid will feel out of balance. The correction for this condition is simply spending more time and energy in the neglected area. When too much time and energy is spent in one part, cutting back on some activities or time spent will alleviate the problem. Here are a few examples of a part being out of balance: (1) too much time playing sports—physical, (2) not processing emotions or letting emotions build up inside—emotional, (3) spending a great deal of time with friends at the expense of other responsibilities—social, and (4) rarely making an effort to learn spiritual truths and values as they relate to the teen's life—spiritual.

If the One-Minute Scolding is used without recognizing the concept of balance, the parent will have a much harder time achieving a desired behavior. On the other hand, a simple and highly productive way to change unwanted behavior is to (1) determine if an area is out of balance and contributing to a specific misbehavior, and then, (2) regulate your teen's activities to achieve balance, and (3) use the One-Minute Scolding for all behavior that needs changing. Remember, your teen needs you to help him learn good habits that promote balance, and he will judge the importance of this concept by the importance you place on your own personal life.

Spiritual Life

No matter which term you use, relating to God, our Creator, a Supreme Being, or a Higher Power is the essence of a spiritual life. Everyone has this capacity, and even small children have an elementary ability. Your teenager's spiritual life has a direct impact on her morals, beliefs, and behavior. Many kids, and even adults, have neglected this area, and the result has been an empty spot that tugs, pulls, and yearns to be filled with a spiritual relationship.

If a teenager has an underdeveloped or nonexistent spiritual identity, she will feel a void in her life. Many times she may try to fill this spiritual void with human relationships, and none of these attempts quite quench the emptiness.

In a teenager, misbehavior may have its roots wholly or partially in the lack of a spiritual identity. Her spiritual life may be out of balance and contributing to a specific behavior such as harmful relationships or annoying dependencies. Where there is misbehavior, the parent should evaluate whether his child's actions are the result of filling this spiritual need inappropriately. When a teen runs out of answers and hope and has no spiritual life to fall back on, she may become disillusioned and despondent. A spiritual life gives her the necessary absolutes that she can count on when life is difficult and when she needs to make important decisions.

To question a young person's spiritual beliefs and inquire about her identity may be quite difficult and unproductive. Yet, if the attitude of the parent is open and supportive, a sharing of beliefs or values may occur and be very beneficial. The youth's beliefs are hard for the parent to change directly, but the best way to do this is to live the example, as kids learn best by example. Please do not use the One-Minute Scolding to make your child believe what you believe. It would be divisive, and it won't work. Rather, use the One-Minute Scolding to reduce the *inappropriate attempts* to fill a spiritual void. It is also appropriate to discipline her when she refuses to participate in the family's religious activities. Discipline behavior, not beliefs. The sooner you start addressing your child's spiritual life, the easier it will be for both of you.

Independence Versus Rebellion

Teenagers are often accused of rebelling against their parents. But more often than not, these adolescents are exercising their independence rather than rebelling. Teens feel an increasing sense of identity separate from mom and dad, and this is a not only normal, but desirable part of the maturing process. They want the benefits of being adults and independent, but they're not quite ready to handle all the responsibilities. We want our kids to be able to provide for their own physical, emotional, and spiritual needs eventually—this is independence. When disciplining your teenager with a One-Minute Scolding, you may experience your son's strong defense of his own views and direction for his life, but this is usually an expression of independence, not rebellion. Independence is a very important goal for your teenager, but you have every right to expect him to obey your rules while living at home. Encourage both the growth of independence *and* conformity with your rules.

Peers Versus Parents

Most teens are surrounded by kids of their own age at school and other social gatherings. Adolescents want to be accepted within a dynamic and energetic peer group because it reinforces their feelings of self-worth. With a lack of acceptance, attention, or even love at home, the influence of peers on these kids is immense. They often get into trouble because they fear ridicule from their peers more than discipline from their parents; sadly, the peer group can become more important than the parents. Most kids don't have the inner strength and endurance to swim against the current of peer pressure because they are usually battling with self-doubt. To help lessen the influence of peers, parents need to give a stronger, more credible "affirming half" of the One-Minute Scolding during discipline. Furthermore, parents need to take a closer look at their life to root out things that diminish their love and increase the need in their teen to seek acceptance elsewhere.

Sensitivity

To be sensitive parents means to be aware of the needs and emotions of their children. Too often a parent is too busy with a career, other children, or other interests to notice and respond to the different needs of each child. In other cases, a parent may treat all the children the same regardless of their individual needs. Paying attention to one child's hobby and not another's is common. Some parents drink alcohol too much, and the result is they are numbed towards their child's needs. Other parents tune out their family with television. The child interprets a lack of attention, or a preference by the parent towards another sibling, as dislike of themselves by the parent. When it comes time to discipline the youth, he may believe that you do not understand him, that your "scolding half" of the One-Minute Scolding is out of touch with the misbehavior, and that your "affirming half" is phony. Parents, ask yourself whether you are truly aware of your child's needs and emotions, and reduce or eliminate obstacles that hinder *your* sensitivity level.

Children from toddlers to teenagers come with different sensitivity levels. The sensitive ones are more easily hurt emotionally because they are highly responsive to what goes on around them. One function of being a parent is to build a child's sense of self-worth and identity. To do this effectively, parents must be aware of their child's sensitivity level. Some sensitive children don't need a lot of discipline because they learn the rules quickly. Others are easily hurt by too intense Scoldings because it only takes a small amount of intensity to upset them. Sensitive youths more often notice when their dad or mom prefers a sibling's hobby or sport over their own. And parents cause big problems with their children when they show no sensitivity towards their children in this respect. For example, a father has three teenage sons. One likes to work on cars, another likes long-distance bicycle racing, and the third likes to paint and do artwork. The father likes to work with tools on cars and spends most of his time helping the first son. The father is a football fan and never shows interest in the second son's bicycling sport. The father is openly critical of the third's son's pursuits and says he will never get a good job doing things like that. The first son is favored because the father spends his time there. The second son is hurt because the father shows no interest in something the boy loves. The third son is angry at the father because the father doesn't understand him, and the father shows no sensitivity towards him. Who do you think responds best to discipline? It's the first son because he is constantly affirmed. The second son doubts his father's love, and thinks the One-Minute Scolding is a waste of time. The last son has numbed his father out because the father causes too much pain. In summary, kids need approval from their parents irrespective of their interests, adjusted to their own sensitivity level, to build their self-esteem and self-worth.

Praise or Criticism

Many teenagers do not receive enough praise for things they do right. Instead, parents just assume that doing right is expected and don't bother to praise them. On the other hand, criticism is easy to dish out when a wrongdoing provokes the parent's anger. Criticism usually represents a higher percentage of the parent's comments, and these have the effect of gradually tearing down a teen's self-worth and self-confidence. Since there is really no right and wrong in trivial matters, why should parents heap criticism on their kid? For non-trivial issues, why not help the youth overcome his shortcomings rather than engaging in fault-finding alone? When a teenager disobeys and the One-Minute Scolding is used, how can he believe the "affirming half" if his life is dominated with parental criticism? During the "scolding half" of the One-Minute Scolding, will a parent's dislike for some of the kid's trivial behavior spill over and show itself as excessive anger or even rage? To make the One-Minute Scolding fair and most effective, praise more and criticize less in everyday life.

Explaining the Rules

When teenagers ask why they can't do something, have you heard or used the response, "Because I said so!"? This statement essentially throws the door shut on further learning about a behavior that the parents believe is wrong. Using this expression may have its time and place, but it doesn't work well with teens. If parents really want to teach their youths, they should explain the background behind each rule. In order to educate, a parent should discuss short and long-term consequences, why the parent's way will lead to a better solution, and the parent's values as they relate to the behavior. Most kids are smart, and they will respond well when they are treated with informative material about a subject.

The prime time to go over the "whys" with your child is after a One-Minute Scolding when your kid asks questions. At other times, always be willing to answer your child's questions. The more truth or facts the kids know, the less likely they are to initiate behavior ignorant of the consequences. Your child will have a mind and a memory full of reasons not to get into trouble. Now it is up to him to keep from misbehaving.

Hypocrisy

We all hate hypocrisy, yet we're slow to see it in ourselves. Hypocrisy means saying or believing one thing and doing another. Maybe you have heard the double message some parents tell their children, "Do as I say, not as I do." If something is bad for the kids to do, how can it be right for the parents? Kids are smart, and they are quick to recognize double standards. Within most children subjected to parental hypocrisy is the thought, "clean up your life before you try to clean up mine!"

If parents are hypocritical, then their discipline (teaching efforts) are flawed because their children will always ask, "Do you really mean what you say?" Hypocrisy and double standards on the part of parents will destroy the effectiveness of the One-Minute Scolding because the kids will not believe someone who doesn't "practice what he teaches." Parents who want their children to believe them need to remove all hints of hypocrisy and double standards.

I'll give you a common example of perceived hypocrisy found in many homes. A father and mother have told their 14-year-old son that he is not to drink alcohol, and that it is not good for him. On weekends, the father drinks a few beers at home while watching a basketball game. The son asks his father, "If I can't drink a beer because it's bad for me, how come you can?" The father responds, "Because I'm old enough, you're not." The youth is confused by this complex message, and he assumes that his dad has double standards. While the confusion in the youth is understandable, a less confusing solution is available. If the father would stop drinking around his son until the boy was old enough to understand alcohol and its potential, the boy would not see this hypocrisy re-enacted every weekend. Parents should avoid even the appearance of hypocrisy for their child's sake.

No Role Model

With a divorce rate of almost fifty percent in the United States, nearly thirty percent of families with children are headed by one parent. Most of these single-parent families are headed by women, but about one-sixth are single fathers raising children. In addition, the number of men caring solely for their children is increasing. Adolescents find themselves being raised by grandparents, aunts and uncles, neighbors, and sometimes even strangers. For many of these teenagers, a same-sex role model is missing at home.

Take for example, a 15-year-old named Michael, who lives with his divorced mother and his 12-year-old brother. Most of Michael's high school teachers are women, the Sunday school teacher is a woman, most of his friends live in homes headed by women, and his girlfriend is another significant female influence. All the discipline comes from his mother now, and Michael begins to resent living in a woman-dominated world. Where does a boy like this get the sense of what it is to be a man? Who is the example for him? Where is the balance? Who can show Michael the way? The same scenario, deficits in same-sex role models, takes place for girls and young women too.

When disciplining an adolescent male using the One-Minute Scolding in an environment dominated by the opposite sex, he is likely to be resentful and rebellious toward the authority. In some cases, the teen may get mad at the parent to the point of acting out in an enraged manner. Underlying all this behavior is the fact that the boy misses his father. He wishes that he heard his father's affirming voice and longs to see how he solves problems in life from day to day. But reality says a hole exists in his needs, and he's not getting what he used to get. To think that the opposite-sex parent can fill all of his needs for same-sex relationships is impossible and even ridiculous.

Several options are available to alleviate this situation. First, the opposite-sex parent must identify misbehavior that is rooted solely in the lack of a same-sex parent or role model. Sometimes, one misbehavior overlaps another in an event, and this requires separating the misbehaviors and disciplining each appropriately. Continue to use the One-Minute Scolding for all misbehaviors, but be sure you discipline for one misbehavior at a time and with appropriate intensity.

When a misbehavior is rooted in the youth's expression of frustration and hurt related to not having a same-sex role model (e.g., screaming and name-calling), and another misbehavior overlaps (e.g., staying out late), the parent needs to see these as two separate misbehaviors—not one. Discipline first for the screaming and name-calling while seeing this behavior as an intense expression of the kid's frustration over missing his same-sex parent—not as anger or rebellion. Next, discipline the youth for staying out late. In each of these two disciplinary acts, remember to keep your scolding proportionate to the "crime," and your affirmations sufficient to his needs.

Second, the teenager should be encouraged to join organizations or activities that are headed by same-sex role models. The parent should meet with the child's surrogate same-sex role model(s) and get to know them. This adult substitution for a missing parent will diminish, but not eliminate, the emotional tug and pull caused by a parent's absence. Consequently, home life and the disciplining process will get easier. Finally, the youth should be encouraged to converse and interact with his same-sex parent whenever wise and possible.

A Parent Not Her Own

When couples separate or divorce, one parent or the other usually takes the children. In some cases, the children split their time between the two parents. Sometime later, one of these parents may remarry, and the children all of a sudden have a "second" mother or father. Rules and disciplining techniques change, and the results can be confusion, resentment, and rebellion in the children and adolescents.

Nobody likes change, least of all the children, and with this change comes symptoms and feelings such as fear and anger. A girl feels alone and misses her biological mother; she doesn't want a new mother. She believes that no surrogate mother can take the place of her real mom. Furthermore, she doesn't like her father pouring out affection to anyone but her real mom. She doesn't like the situation at all.

To bring peace and harmony into the new family structure, the youth's new set of parents must agree on the rules and on a disciplinary approach. The One-Minute Scolding stands ready to fill this void. It is readily understood and implemented, and it has been tested and used by thousands of parents and child caretakers.

When using the One-Minute Scolding, the child's resistance to the method is likely to be composed of two parts. First, she doesn't like being disciplined, and second, she doesn't think her stepmother is qualified to discipline her. After repeated One-Minute Scoldings, the child will lessen her distaste for the situation and trust the stepmom if, and only if, she disciplines consistently and fairly, making sure she gives her stepdaughter honest affirmations in the second half of the One-Minute Scolding.

After all, the stepmother is now a parent, and she should be encouraged to overcome her reluctance to discipline her new stepchild as if she was her own biological child. The girl needs to know the new boundaries or rules of the stepparent, and discipline is an important tool for teaching this behavior. No discipline by the stepmother means that she is not assuming the full role as parent. Worse yet, a lack of discipline by the stepparent may be interpreted by the child as indifference and a lack of caring.

The child doesn't have to like the stepmother right away, but she does have to obey her rules. In time, a relationship will form between the child and the stepparent, but it will not be the same as between the child and her biological parent. Furthermore, the child should be encouraged to have some form of relationship with her biological mother whenever wise and possible, and this should ease the sense of losing the relationship with her mother that she once had.

While the girl is in the home of her new stepparent, she must be told to obey rules belonging to her new set of parents rather than rules of her previous set of parents. When the child visits her biological parent, the rules may change at that household; the child may be permitted to do things that she couldn't do at home. When she goes over to her biological mother's house, the girl will be expected to obey that household's rules. Although somewhat difficult and not always possible, common rules should be agreed upon so that discipline is consistent, making it easier on the child and the parents.

Situations like those just mentioned can be quite complex for separated or divorced parents to solve, so don't hesitate to seek some impartial advice through professional help in the form of family counseling. Being separated from a parent is painful, frustrating, and bewildering for any child or adolescent. So be patient, encourage your children to express their feelings about the situation, and spend a lot of fun time with your kid(s).

Harmful Self-Gratification

Today's youths often complain that they are bored and lack excitement. Others have real deficits of love and attention because both their parents work and stay busy when at home. When these two situations combine in teenagers, the kids usually "get into trouble" while attempting to meet their own needs. Meeting needs the wrong way still leaves kids feeling needy.

From many avenues, teenagers are being taught that "if it feels good, do it." And we hear them say that if it feels good, it must be a good thing to do. These kids put off the rewards associated with waiting for something for immediate gratification with unpleasant consequences. Many adolescents take the easy way out only to find that their life has been made more difficult in the long run. Kids try more and more things in an attempt to feel good about themselves. This escalation in misbehavior may lead to immorality or other harmful behavior. When kids finally experience inevitable unpleasant consequences, they try to mask their sadness, loneliness, and disappointment by numbing them out with more intense feelings brought about by sex, drugs, music, risky behavior, etc. And some youths overwhelmed by the stress of all this behavior may choose to join over a million adolescents in the United States who drop out of high school. In the end, the youth has made a mess and will require the help of others, possibly even professionals, to straighten his life out. But there is an alternative to ending in pain and despair.

How does a parent use the One-Minute Scolding to discipline misbehavior associated with seeking intense, pleasurable feelings in harmful ways? The parent does three things. First, explain the natural consequences of misbehavior intensely and clearly. Second, re-evaluate the rules, and establish reasonable boundaries and limits where needed for the teen's protection. And third, fight a feeling with a feeling. If the child wants intense positive feelings, you provide an intense "affirming half" in a One-Minute Scolding when discipline is necessary. At other times, "love the stuffing" out of your kid, and he or she won't feel the need to go elsewhere looking for love in all the wrong places.

"Hormones on Two Legs"

Most teenagers feel or act as if their sexual desires were in charge of their body's actions. As a rule, teens have a significant interest in sexual matters, and all adults can relate to this because they were teens at one time too. Sexual attractions are meant to empower teenagers to seek out relationships, and they are normal and natural if kept within their proper boundaries.

Sexual energy is like atomic energy. Use it right and it can be beneficial and translate into great amounts of energy. Sexual activity bonds one person to another, and teenagers usually experience this with intensity. Use sexual energy unwisely, and it can be highly destructive. Many teens are deceived by the pleasure of sex and the "hunt" for it, thinking that because it feels good, it must be good. They also fail to see the consequences of misuse until something unforeseen or ignored happens.

For the majority of teenagers engaging in sexual relationships, a painful end to a relationship comes before the first anniversary of their sexual activity. When strong relationship bonds formed through sexual activity are broken, anger, despair, loneliness, and fear sweep through the young person's life in massive quantities. Long-term damage from sexual activity, whether infrequent, promiscuous, or "faithful to another," can be done in a teen's life in the form of frightening diseases, difficulty in forming future attachments, and unwanted pregnancies (four out of ten teenage girls will become pregnant). And we should stress that today, sex can be deadly.

If you discipline your teenager for disobeying a rule related to sexual activity, remember that sexual desires in a teenager will most likely be stronger than any One-Minute Scolding. Once kids start having sex, they rarely stop. However, you should continue disciplining your kids when they break your rules regarding sex. You should explain the natural consequences of their behavior, and encourage either abstinence or a healthier use of sex. Insist on responsible behavior. For sure, the One-Minute Scolding can promote better communication between you and your teen, and your teenager needs your openness, honesty, and guidance as it relates to sex and sexuality.

Drugs and Addiction

Too many adolescents and pre-adolescents experiment with illegal drugs such as marijuana, hallucinogens (LSD, PCP, etc.), inhalants, cocaine, "crack," methamphetamines, sedatives, and/or alcohol. Far too often, these kids keep using their favorite drug until they become regular users. Parents do not want their kids to use drugs, and this includes parents who experimented with drugs themselves as teenagers in the 1960s or 1970s. But how much is too much? And when does "just saying no" to drugs and alcohol apply? When is there a problem?

Most parents think they know if their kid is using drugs, but most really don't. Teens who experiment are usually not noticed, but regular users usually show signs that a perceptive parent could see. A teenager who is using drugs usually displays a life out of balance, a concept discussed previously. A parent might notice an unkempt appearance, a change in clothing style, a weight loss, changes in sleep patterns, too little or too much sleep. The teen becomes moody and irritable, or even depressed. Socially, the teen may drop his regular friends, add undesirable friends, increase or begin sexual activity, drop out of school or talk about it, and react differently to family members. Spiritually, he may express changed values or morals and become defensive about them, refuse to go to religious activities that he once did, and radically change his beliefs about how he fits into life and about his future. Take a close look at these four areas, and if you see your child in this situation, you have a big problem.

First, we must recognize that two types of drug users exist. One type can put the drugs down and walk away, never to return. The One-Minute Scolding will be effective for this type of situation involving casual use of drugs because the youth still has the ability to say no. The key to this is spotting it early. The more involved with your kid you are, the more likely you will see the small changes in his life associated with drug use and experimentation.

The other type of drug user cannot put drugs down and walk away because he is addicted and has lost his ability to choose. Getting the youth to admit that there is a problem with drugs will be a big challenge—denial is prevalent. This teen's life has become unmanageable, and neither he nor you can manage his life now. For an addicted adolescent, you will need more tools than the One-Minute Scolding provides to change his undesirable conduct, but you should continue to use the discipline method since your rules are being broken. You may wish to draw new boundaries and create new rules as a step towards protecting your child from the consequences of his misbehavior, but you should not stop there. As an addition to discipline, prompt professional help skilled in the treatment of chemically dependent adolescents is a must because the family and the drug user do not have the answers to addiction within themselves. If left without parental and family intervention, the drug-addicted youth may end up with legal trouble, in an institution, or even dead. Don't wait; the problem won't go away.

Wounds That Speak

Some children and adolescents have been wounded by abuse from a parent, a neighbor, a friend, a boyfriend, a teacher, or even a stranger. This abuse may be sexual, physical, or emotional and can happen at any point in a youth's life. The actual act of abuse may occur on just one day or over weeks, months, and even years. Too often, parents don't recognize the signs of abuse because they don't want to admit that it has happened to one they love, and/or they assign the signs of abuse to some other cause.

Some important signs of abuse towards children and adolescents are: unexplained bruises and scratches, reluctance to be with someone they know, exhibiting inappropriate affection, sudden use of sexual terminology, discomfort with affection, sleep problems such as sleeplessness or nightmares, not wanting to sleep alone or in the dark, depression, anxiety, withdrawal, moodiness, personality changes, and new problems in school.

Children and adolescents don't want to talk about abuse because they are embarrassed, feel that no one really understands, are afraid of retaliation, or think that it was their fault. It takes a special parent with superb sensitivity to communicate with these youths about the abuse. These secrets require a lot of energy on the part of the victim to keep them hidden. These secrets and the pain associated with them are the fuel for misbehaviors in the young person's life.

The One-Minute Scolding is a disciplining tool applicable to all misbehaviors, but a parent may experience great difficulty while using the One-Minute Scolding with an abused child, when just a month prior no difficulty existed. The kid may be overly sensitive to the "scolding half," and shy away from affection in the second half. Also, the abused kid may tune the parent out, or react with a fit of anger. In every case, you'll see a definite change in the way the One-Minute Scolding is received. Parents who discover or suspect abuse rarely have the tools necessary for helping their kid. Going outside of the family for help ensures that the proper actions are taken. Furthermore, professionals are qualified to teach the parents how to help their child in the best way. Be patient and listen carefully to your child. Maintain an attitude of unconditional love and acceptance, and your child will recover as quickly as possible. Keep your eyes and ears open.

Unusual Persistent Moods or Behaviors

When the One-Minute Scolding has been administered correctly a number of times, your teenager still may not have changed his behavior. He may have a good home environment and admirable peers, but still, something appears to be wrong. The answer may be that your child has the beginnings of a mental or emotional disorder such as depression, anxiety, hyperactivity, or a learning disorder. These conditions usually interfere with the child's ability to respond to the One-Minute Scolding and to follow your rules.

Even if your adolescent wanted to follow your rules, the beginnings of an illness may not allow him to. If your son is somewhat depressed, he may say that he is too tired to do his chores when he is supposed to. In school, your son's teacher may complain to you that the boy cannot sit still and be quiet. The teen may experience days or weeks of anxiety for no apparent reason and limit his activity as a way of coping. Efforts to change a behavior without knowing an illness exists will be fruitless.

Since very few parents have the answers needed to solve complex behavioral situations resulting from mental or emotional disorders, they need to seek professional help for their child. Be compassionate and reassure your child that you will help him solve these difficulties.

Parents may feel slightly guilty or repulsed by the fact that their child has the beginnings of a mental or emotional disorder. Once a diagnosis is made, parents must become educated about an illness, as better understanding will greatly diminish the stigma. Mom, Dad, look deep inside your teenager. He is the same as he ever was, but his personality is being masked by his illness. And most importantly, know that most of these problems can be treated with professional help. Be the person in your teen's life who leads him to health. Be strong, take the initiative, and start today.

Expectations and Disappointments

How many parents raise their children with expectations that they will go to college, play certain sports, follow a certain career, have a fun, dynamic life, or have interests and hobbies just the same as their own? In life, we find that each kid is unique and has different talents, abilities, and even physical characteristics. Sometimes a parent may share a common interest or preference with their child or adolescent, but it is highly unlikely that the parent and the child are just alike. When the parent's expectations for the youth aren't met, the result can be disappointment. When the same parent disciplines using the One-Minute Scolding, he or she may be too negative or critical rather than affirming. At other times, the parent may not care enough to discipline a child whose life is displeasing. The judgment that the young person is wrong for having different interests, hobbies, or physical attributes must not enter the One-Minute Scolding. Drop your expectations and let your son or daughter make the most of his or her talents and abilities.

Types of Professionals and Caregivers

Lots of problems can arise for a child or adolescent, but fortunately these problems can be dealt with. Listings for psychological, psychiatric, and neuropsychological services may be found in the yellow pages of most phone books. Help is available for treating and managing school problems, learning disabilities, hyperactivity, attention deficits, dyslexia, abuse of all types, alcohol and drug abuse, eating disorders, troubled relationships, self-esteem issues, anxiety, phobias, depression, stress, compulsive habits, grief, trauma, and parenting skills. The following is a partial list of the types of child care providers, and most are within financial reach of everyone.

* Social workers (MSWs)
* Child psychologists (PhDs)
* Child psychiatrists (Medical Doctors or M.D.s)
* School counselors
* Counseling centers for adolescents
* Hospitals specializing in adolescents and children
* Clergy specializing in youth ministries
* Law enforcement personnel
* Parent support groups
* Classes for learning parenting skills
* A support group centered on the application of the One-Minute Scolding. Why not start one in your area?

Now that we have discussed many of the major influences on adolescents and even children, you have the more difficult task of applying what you read. Some of the areas in this chapter are more difficult to follow through on than others, but all can be done. Your best efforts, one day at a time, will convince the teenager to choose good behavior as the norm. Persistence pays off. Finally, keep applying the One-Minute Scolding through the good times and the bad, always seeking progress rather than perfection in your son or daughter.

Chapter 11

Responding to Challenges from Your Children

Charming and docile as they may be, your children are not going to roll over and play dead when you discipline them. They have a whole arsenal of clever defenses, so you had better be prepared with some "creative" responses.

Let's look in on some scenes of parents disciplining their children, paying particular attention to the defenses the children use and what the parent does to "neutralize" those defenses.

Wiggling

In an effort to test your conviction and your strength, some small children will squirm and wiggle and slip off your lap like a fish to the floor. But the disciplining process cannot begin until the child is firmly restrained by the parent.

Through age six or seven, the One-Minute Scolding is best begun with the child on your lap. You don't need to work out with weights to be strong enough for this youngster. In truth, she is only like a "slippery fish" who needs to be held on your lap. Here's what you need to do. Neither the youngster nor her spirit will be hurt or broken; it will only relieve her to know that you are indeed strong enough to handle her.

Grasp her by the upper arms, place her on your lap, lock her in place by putting your leg over hers, hold her hands, and proceed with the One-Minute Scolding.

Howling

Some youngsters may cry and wail and scream as though they were being beaten—and all you did so far was begin the "scolding" half of the One-Minute Scolding. It may cause your spouse to run in alarm, but no one is hurt.

You do not want to start a screaming match to have your "scolding" heard over the youngster's howling. Instead, surprise him by giving him permission to do exactly what he is already doing. "Go ahead, Matt. You feel bad, and you should feel bad. So I want you to cry, very hard. Get it out of your system. I'll just hold you and wait. When you finish, I'll go on with the Scolding."

Matt may find it difficult to carry on and on with loud howls just to delay the inevitable return to the Scolding. After all, you are still holding him, and it is clear that you are willing to wait for days if necessary. His out-of-proportion shrieking will not ruffle your patience nor drown your determination. Neither have you set yourself up for another match with him to determine "who is the boss around here." Had you fallen for his ploy and demanded silence so that he could hear the Scolding, you would have only escalated the match which, indeed, you probably would have lost. So, save yourself the frustration. Insist that he wail louder, and he will find himself an obedient son, howling at your command. Or, more likely, he will quiet down.

When you know that he can hear you, proceed with the One-Minute Scolding. If Matt finds it necessary to check your determination and patience again with another crack at wailing, encourage him. "Go ahead, Matt, you still feel awful. Cry as hard as you need to. Get it out of your system." When he is finished, you resume the Scolding just where you left off. Matt isn't stupid. He will see that his behavior has only prolonged the inevitable. Besides, it's a great relief to him to know that you mean to hang in there with him.

Shutting Out

Melissa sits on her mother's lap and is being disciplined. Suddenly, she is inspired to put her finger in her ears and squeeze her eyes shut. She does not like what she hears and sees. You take her fingers out of her ears very calmly, and hold her hands in yours. You know you cannot open her eyes. Melissa turns her face away, squeezes her eyes shut even tighter and pulls as far away from you as she can. No problem. Melissa can still hear you even if she cannot see you.

Proceed with the Scolding, first the angry part and then the part that tells her how you love her and want her not to misbehave anymore. Your message will come through loud and clear. She will hear the feelings in your voice and feel them in your hug. Melissa will know you are loving and strong enough to cope with her attempts to avoid discipline. You have promised her that you will always discipline her when she makes a mistake, no matter what, and you will always love her, no matter what.

Apparent Indifference

Elizabeth is nine years old and tough. It has come to her father's attention that she has told a bold-faced lie. He begins the One-Minute Scolding and though he is really quite irritated and angry and his voice clearly expresses it, Elizabeth has focused her gaze coolly some place in the area of his tie pin and remains totally unruffled.

If you were Elizabeth's father, you must remember to persevere. No need to get frantic and raise your voice. Remain exactly as angry as you feel and proceed with the Scolding. Elizabeth's cool imperturbability is designed to make you feel ineffectual. Believe me, if she can hear you, she is having intense feelings.

As the One-Minute Scolding is concluded with the warm promise of care and helpfulness, her father gives her a hug, and suddenly Elizabeth bursts into tears.

"No one loves me," she sobs. Suddenly, there is a discharge of feeling, and the little girl shows how very sad she really has been feeling. The stony, glazed look was her effort to keep all this sadness locked in where no one would touch it. Her father is present and ready with his warmth and understanding.

Feeling Mistreated

Ryan, who is eleven, has taken twenty dollars from his visiting grandmother's purse. You are very angry and upset with him. Your One-Minute Scolding states this clearly and furthermore, restitution is to be made. In the Scolding you offer a very clear plan as to how this restitution is to be made, and you also promise to help him carry it out.

"Ryan, because I love you and want to help you solve this problem, I will advance you twenty dollars from your allowance to pay Grandma back. We will go to Grandma, and I will give you courage to ask her forgiveness and tell her it won't happen again."

The One-Minute Scolding is not yet finished when Ryan interrupts with the complaint that he's always the one who gets into trouble in this house. He angrily states that you never discipline his sister. He tries to convince you that he is the family scapegoat and make you feel guilty for it.

Do not deal with any of these issues until after the Scolding is complete. After the hug, encourage him to talk about his feelings of being mistreated. Encourage him to say how sad and angry he must feel for being "scolded" more often than his sister.

Do not tell him that his feelings are inappropriate, or that it is wrong to feel mistreated. Listen carefully without interruption, and encourage him to discharge everything until he is finished.

"Ryan, it's too bad you feel so mistreated. I'm sorry, and I certainly don't want to be unfair. But I will discipline you every time you misbehave because I love you and want to be a helpful mom. If you misbehave more often than your sister, you'll have to be disciplined more often. If I ever discipline you for anything other than misbehavior or a broken rule, please tell me. I surely want to be fair with you, Ryan."

Pressing Your Buttons and Verbal Retorts

Daniel is a powerful player, and he needs to be disciplined even if he is a strapping thirteen. An agreement was made that this Saturday it was his turn to straighten things up and sweep. Instead, he left the garage in a mess, and took off with his buddies for the afternoon. Later, his mother catches him by the sleeve as he saunters into the kitchen, holds his arm, and tells him that he's due for a One-Minute Scolding. She feels a little awkward about the discipline formula, and as she takes a breath to begin, Daniel is inspired to cash in on her awkward feelings.

"Great," he says, "I love this. The boiled egg scolding, leaves ya a little soft in the head but . . . Could I get you a timer, perhaps your little recipe book, so that you do me just right, not too hard, not too runny? Mom, you've got to be kidding. This is one big waste of time."

His mother interrupts, "It certainly is, Daniel. If you'll save your words for afterwards, you won't prolong the minute. I'll be glad to hear how angry you are when I'm finished, but your sarcasm won't protect you from getting a One-Minute Scolding."

Proceed and complete the entire Scolding. Afterwards, invite him to share his feelings.

Emancipating

When teenagers practice their independence they may try breaking a rule here and there. But pretending to be fully emancipated does not mean that there are no consequences for those broken rules.

As the mother or father, one cannot afford to "look the other way." Your authority is being directly challenged, but remember, down deep, your teenager does not want you to relinquish it, no matter how testy she is. You want her to become independent eventually, but she must obey your rules along that pathway to independence and adulthood.

Michelle, at sixteen, has just arrived home an hour and a half late from an excursion with the family car.

Both parents stand at the door to receive her. As Michelle knows what to expect, she pushes past them defiantly and heads down the hallway to her room saying, "Look, I don't need any of your lectures and one-minute routines. I'd much rather you just told me to stay home instead of going through all that stuff."

No problem. Her parents trundle off down the hall behind her. Her father begins the One-Minute Scolding as they walk toward her room. If she interrupts again with sarcasm, ridicule, or defiance, they simply wait until she finishes and then proceed with the Scolding. Her dad knows not to get caught in a shouting match, so as Michelle raises her voice dramatically, her dad just responds ever more quietly and waits to resume the Scolding. When the full minute of discipline is up, each parent again reminds Michelle how much they love her and leave quietly. Discipline is over.

More than anything else, children want to be absolutely certain that you are strong enough for them and love them enough to stand by them. No matter what kind of defenses your youngsters use, you will reach them effectively if you are absolutely firm in your delivery and completion of the One-Minute Scolding. Deliver it exactly as prescribed, thirty seconds of high-level "negative" emotion, a deep breath, then the abrupt downhill course of thirty seconds that are intensely warm, loving, supportive, and present. Have courage. Persistence pays off.

Chapter 12

Answers to Common Questions

After being introduced to the One-Minute Scolding or after using it for a time, some parents encounter circumstances or responses that cause them difficulties. We are passing along these experiences, both good and bad, to help in understanding what does and what does not work. This sampling of questions has come from parents and teachers and will help clarify the Scolding for you.

Q: What if I use the One-Minute Scolding and it doesn't work? When my child continues to misbehave, what do I do?

A: The first thing you must ask yourself is, "Am I giving the whole One-Minute Scolding, or am I administering only part of it? Am I giving it the prescribed way?"

One mother who has been using the Scolding with real success for a year told me that she had caught herself disciplining her son one night and wondered why it wasn't working. She was preparing some snacks for guests who were about to arrive and was rather involved in the process.

The little fellow kept coming out of bed to see if the guests had arrived yet, and might he help chop this or that, and chattering about nothing. Well, she wanted him off and in bed. It was late, and he had had a story and his usual night-time rituals. So she told him to hustle back to bed and go to sleep—now! When he padded out to kitchen for the fifth time, she realized that things weren't working.

She told me that she then washed her hands and reviewed her tactics, only to discover she'd indeed given her message about getting back to bed, but she had not taken enough time to convey how seriously she felt about this, and how really annoyed she was with his reappearances.

Second, she had not taken enough time with the second half of the Scolding either! Her son felt only shunted off, not loved or good about himself.

Third, she had forgotten to touch or hold or hug him because of her greasy fingers. She told me that as soon as she had done the One-Minute Scolding completely and properly with all of its parts and in the right order, and had touched and held him, it was over. He scurried right off and went to bed.

This mother's experience is quite typical. When you use the One-Minute Scolding properly, it works. If you find that the One-Minute Scolding isn't working, you may find it very useful to read the review in Chapter 13 and look at the structure of the Scolding itself. Be sure that you use it entirely and correctly.

Q: My child is tough. What should I do when she shows no signs of feeling upset? Should I go on expressing my anger until she does?

A: No. The first half of the Scolding should last no more than thirty seconds. You are not going to solve all your disciplinary problems with some children in the first thirty seconds.

Most children need several Scoldings before a change occurs, but each Scolding should be kept within the prescribed time limit.

Q: During the first half of the Scolding, if my child cries right away do I still have to go on and on with the scolding half?

A: When you see that your child is feeling upset, you have scolded him enough. It is not how long you scold your child (although it should never be longer than thirty seconds), but rather how clearly you scold him and how intensely you express your real feelings during the scolding half that count. You want your child to feel your sadness, your anger, your annoyance, your frustration, and/or whatever feeling you have about his misbehavior.

Probably better than anyone else, you know when your child is having feelings. From the slight changes in his facial expression, a tightness around his mouth, a sad look or tears in his eyes, or perhaps the dropping of his head, you can detect the changes in his feelings. As soon as you see that your child is feeling upset, stop. You have given him your message and the first half of the One-Minute Scolding is over.

Q: Why shouldn't I use additional punishments along with the One-Minute Scolding. Wouldn't that work faster?

A: No. It isn't necessary and it doesn't work. Punishment in any form tends to elicit anger and resentment from your children and this interferes with their learning new and acceptable behaviors. Discipline such as the One-Minute Scolding may also be very uncomfortable for your child, but your intention is to teach rather than to hurt. Your child will feel the difference and respond accordingly.

Q: Are you saying that the only discipline that I need to use with my child is a Scolding?

A: Yes. One of the advantages of the Scolding method is that when it is over, it is over. It is less work, and it is more effective. Natural consequences should be allowed to happen if they are not hurtful, because they teach your child as well. You may want to discuss the matter further, but more in terms of exploring his or your feelings as well as helping you and your child gain more information so as to handle that particular situation in a more mature and adaptive manner.

Q: What if I feel only slightly annoyed with my child, but think that I will make a greater impact on her if I am angry? Should I try to act angry during the first part of the Scolding?

A: No. Express only what you really feel. Don't role-play. Your honest feelings will make a much stronger impression on your child. They know when you're being honest with them. Remember, the Scolding is more than a disciplinary method; it is a means of communicating with your child, and of developing a better relationship, a relationship that is based on truth and trust. After the fact, your child will remember your honesty and will continue to trust you. The more honest you are as a parent, the more successful you will be with your children.

Q: What should I do if I feel I've just made a big mistake in trying to discipline one of my children? Let's say that I have sent my child away, and I refused to talk to her?

A: I think it is very useful for parents to make mistakes. It provides them with a wonderful opportunity to teach their children how to deal with their mistakes.

As soon as you realize you've made a mistake, go to your child and say, "I'm sorry. I made a mistake. Instead of helping you with your problem, I sent you away and refused to talk to you. Will you forgive me?"

You will be surprised and touched at how readily your child responds in a loving and forgiving manner. Your willingness to admit to a mistake and ask forgiveness will not be forgotten and you may well hear your words and actions return to you in the following weeks.

Q: **I really have trouble seeing myself going home and using this idea because it feels like "the answer." I figure my kids will soon catch on to it as a pat formula that needs to be tuned out.**

A: You are right—the One-Minute Scolding has a prescribed formula that is a big hurdle at first for many people. It makes them feel controlled, as if their own creativity is being suppressed.

When we teach people how to use the One-Minute Scolding, we are teaching an answer. Just as teaching children the multiplication table is teaching "the answers," the ritualized approach of the One-Minute Scolding assures us that we have all the parts necessary to get to the best answer. It doesn't leave you with any blank spaces. The balance is inherent in the ritual and produces a true and effective answer. It's a good ritual because all of the parts are there. You don't have to run around finding the right pieces. That's already been done. It works whether you understand it or not. But there is no doubt at all that you'll like it better when you "know it in your bones." Then you have made it your own. When you see how it works and appreciate it, you'll be very creative in your interactions with your children. Then you will be able to keep your feeling expressions balanced without feeling as if you are using a formula.

Q: I find it difficult to stop scolding after only thirty seconds and act warm and loving when I am still very angry. Isn't that being hypocritical?

A: Many people ask that question as they learn to use the One-Minute Scolding. Remember, we use adult skills and strengths to express anger adaptively and to stop expressing negative feelings at the end of thirty seconds. This is challenging but relatively easy to learn with practice. At the end of those first angry thirty seconds or less, take that deep breath and remind yourself that you do not stop loving your child when you are angry and upset with her. You're not lying to her when you express your love in the second half of the Scolding. You do love her. You do know that she is a good person. You know she will learn other ways of behaving. You know that you'll never stop being her parent. Her behavior or your anger do not make her a bad person or an unloved child. You're angry and upset at her behavior, not her person. That's not hypocritical, that is maturity.

Q: Won't my expression of anger frighten my daughter and cause her to bottle up her own feelings?

A: Most parents can safely express the full force of their anger to their children without harming them. Fathers probably should "hold back" a bit as their anger can seem more frightening and overwhelming to children. Most mothers when using the Scolding can give full vent to their rage without overwhelming their older children. Obviously, infants and small children cannot cope with the full expression of adult anger.

Using the Scolding gives parents a way of expressing anger in a mature and helpful way. It is also a way of teaching children how to express anger. One mother is a social worker who helps other parents learn how to use the One-Minute Scolding, but when using it personally she gave the following example:

"When we adopted Sarah, a five-year-old Korean orphan girl, I began to use the Scolding in my own home. She was having trouble adjusting and was misbehaving. Her behavior improved considerably and I really have not had to use it much in the last few years. But I think that the biggest payoff has been what it has taught her about herself.

"Unfortunately, my husband and I are divorcing and things have been difficult for all of us. But in the middle of this trying time, I couldn't help but smile when my daughter came up to me and said, 'Mother, I am angry. You and daddy are getting divorced. It's not fair. I am very angry!' I could almost hear myself over the years saying, 'Sarah, I am angry. You did such and such . . . and I am angry!'

"As much as it hurt me to see her so upset I was pleased to see that my daughter wasn't holding back the way I did when I was a child. I know that since I've started to use the Scolding to express my own feelings, that I feel much better about myself and about her."

Q: What if I do not discipline my child every time she misbehaves? If I am inconsistent, will the One-Minute Scolding still work for me?

A: The more consistent you are, the better behaved your child will be, and the better your relationship will be. Use the One-Minute Scolding as often as you can when your child misbehaves. But don't worry about it when you don't. Remember, the One-Minute Scolding isn't asking for "perfection," it is asking for your best effort. It is better for your daughter if you do scold her every time she makes a mistake. But sometimes it is just impossible for you to even spend that one moment. Give yourself a break. The One-Minute Scolding is designed to make parenting easier, not more difficult.

Q: How important is it for me, as a father, to get involved with the discipline? Can I leave it up to my wife because she is better at this sort of thing anyway?

A: Many men have a difficult time expressing feelings, especially warm and tender feelings.

The One-Minute Scolding is almost as important for the father as it is for his youngsters who need to be disciplined. The One-Minute Scolding allows parents to practice both feelings—the angry, annoyed, and irritated ones as well as the warm and loving feelings. Although parents may feel a bit clumsy and embarrassed using the One-Minute Scolding in the beginning, they will find that this method is a way for them to practice expressing themselves fully and completely, as well as appropriately.

"Wait until your father gets home" is fortunately a dying expression in households today. We are purging ourselves of some of those old stereotypes of tough dad/soft mom roles. But in many cases, we've only reversed them. Now we are seeing tough mothers/soft fathers, and that won't work either. So the One-Minute Scolding is like practicing scales on the piano. You practice the right hand and the left hand. It's no longer seen as excusable to leave the other scales for someone else to play.

If the mother jumps in and tries to balance out the father, she'll deprive the dad of a complete expression of feelings and deprive him of the opportunity to develop a close, warm relationship with his children. We all tend to be at least a little lopsided in our abilities to express feelings. That's why the One-Minute Scolding is a great exercise for parents. You may be clumsy at first, but it will teach you balance. It is also very important for children, both boys and girls, to hear their dads express feelings and express them honestly, completely, and appropriately. Parents need to encourage each other to keep practicing.

Q: Should I warn my child first before I actually give her a Scolding? Should I give her another chance?

A: No. Either discipline your child when she misbehaves, or don't discipline your child. A threat only suggests that you may, in fact, not discipline your child for a misbehavior that has already occurred.

Q: What if someone tells me that my child has misbehaved, should I give him a Scolding?

A: No. Discipline him for misbehaviors that you've observed or that you are very certain have occurred. However, it is important that you talk to your child about the misbehavior that's been reported to you. This gives you as a parent a good opportunity to help your child deal with the problem that occurred outside of the home.

Q: What if my child needs to tell me something during the Scolding? Isn't it important for children to express their feelings and for parents to listen to them?

A: During the Scolding it is important that you do not get drawn into a discussion. It is a minute of discipline, not a time for discussion. There is a proper time and place for listening to your child, but the middle of the Scolding is neither the time nor the place. After you have finished and given him a hug or a loving touch, encourage him to express his feelings or discuss the pertinent issues. Then it is important to listen carefully and with respect. Encourage his discharge of feeling so that the two of you are at peace with one another. Don't get caught in a verbal war or argument. If he expresses his feelings inappropriately, he is not necessarily misbehaving. Remember, you are the adult, so you can cope with his feelings in a mature manner.

Q: I thought my child's feelings were the most important thing.

A: Feelings are important. Helping your child express feelings in an appropriate manner is equally important.

Frustrating the wishes of a child for her own good is a loving gesture that parents can make. Don't mix up wishes, whims, or power plays with feelings. If you give into a child's every wish you do not help him learn to deal with reality. The outside world is not so indulgent.

Q: How does this method of discipline compare with behavior modification, where the child is disciplined (or taught) by having to experience the consequences of her own actions?

A: The One-Minute Scolding is compatible with behavior modification. One of the unpleasant consequences of your daughter's misbehavior may be the Scolding she gets from you. You can, of course, also let her experience the other natural consequences of her actions.

If your daughter leaves her bike out on the lawn, despite repeated warnings that it will be stolen if she doesn't put it into the garage, you can give her an understanding response when her bicycle is stolen, but good discipline includes pointing out to her the consequences of her misbehavior. Your child does not need a Scolding or any other kind of discipline because she will feel very upset about losing her bike. If you try to scold or discipline her further, your child loses the beneficial experience of "natural consequences." She has lost her bicycle and must replace it.

Q: What if I use the method but my husband doesn't? Will it still work?

A: Yes. One parent using the One-Minute Scolding consistently is better than neither parent disciplining the child effectively. However, it is far better if each parent is supporting the other by using the same method of discipline.

A child is in a serious situation if one or both parents undermines the other when disciplining the child. Single parents who use the One-Minute Scolding effectively prove their ability to raise a youngster without a partner, even if it would be easier and more effective to have two parents participate. Separated parents should agree on common rules and limits as well as using a discipline familiar to all. This reduces the tensions and troubles that can arise when children live in different homes with separated parents.

Q: Can I use the One-Minute Scolding in public places, or is it better to wait until we get home?

A: Let's say your youngster misbehaves in the supermarket. The supermarket is actually a great place to use the One-Minute Scolding. Back him up against the canned goods, nose-to-nose, whispering intensely and glaring angrily into his little eyes.

After fifteen to twenty seconds of hissed scolding, most children are very relieved to have you relax and smile. Use the Scolding consistently, and he will behave well in public places, supermarkets, or restaurants. Remember that it is the certainty of discipline that prevents misbehavior.

Q: What should I do if my child misbehaves when it really is inconvenient to discipline her at that moment?

A: You are the parent and have the power to decide when and where you discipline your child. If it is inconvenient to discipline her at the moment, give her a look or tell her "I'll talk to you later about this," and forget it for the moment. However, it is important that you remember to discipline your child at a later time when it is more convenient.

However, the more often you choose not to discipline your child in a certain situation, the more likely you are to have a problem with your child in that circumstance. I know a parent who used the Scolding very successfully with her child except in one area. Whenever she was on the phone, her three-year-old would misbehave. The child was taking advantage of the fact that her mom was preoccupied. The more important the phone call, the more likely it was the child would misbehave.

Suddenly the mother saw the light, and she made an important change. The next time she was on the phone and her child began to misbehave, she interrupted her telephone conversation and said, "I'm sorry. My daughter needs my help. I'll call you right back, in fact in two minutes." She spent the next minute administering the complete Scolding. There were a few more interrupted phone calls, but in a week the problem was over.

Q: I rarely need to use the One-Minute Scolding with my son anymore because he hardly ever misbehaves. But I actually miss that chance it gave me for the intense, positive interaction which felt so good to me. What can I do to get that again?

A: That's a very important point. You'll have to create them. Parents don't always have enough routine time to be around their kids as it is. You may want to make a special point of seeking out reasons to be positive and warm with your son by praising him for all those things he does well, answering the phone so nicely, picking up his room, even walking and looking well. Don't forget to just express how nice it feels for you to be his father. Use a physical expression of positive feelings to intensify those words, such as patting, holding, hugging, tugging, and tussling with your children.

There are some youngsters who find it particularly hard to respond to your positive feelings. They don't easily feel your love. I advise those parents to "pounce on your kid!" Children should be surprised and embraced in a big bear hug without warning but with warm, intense feelings of love and affection.

At first those kids think, "Oh, oh, I've been found out." They fear that you've found out one of the many things they've done for which they should be disciplined. So they actually interpret your surprising embrace as trouble. Imagine their relief and joy when you say, "I just wanted you to know how much I love you."

Q: How can I use the principles of the One-Minute Scolding in my classroom? Do I want my students to bond to me as their teacher?

A: Look at it this way: Remember when you were a kid—do you remember any adults or especially a teacher at school who thought you were a wonderful youngster? Was there one in particular who liked you and whom you looked forward to being around? Unfortunately for many youngsters, memories of pleasant adults will be rare. But those who have had such special adults are very grateful for them.

When a teacher takes even a few minutes to relate to each student personally and warmly and just as positively as she does negatively, she gives that child a gift that lasts a lifetime. Teachers, like parents, represent authority, security, warmth, nurture, and care, as well as information. When a teacher creates a secure place free of worry and tension, she reduces anxiety for the student and in that way frees the student to learn.

Actually, attachments can form quickly between students and teachers. Teaching implies a kind of partnership. The process of teaching and learning calls forth a whole range of feelings on both sides of the partnership. If you praise, encourage, and nurture the students, attachments form.

Kids who misbehave give their teacher an opportunity to form attachments to them because the teacher can employ a form of the One-Minute Scolding. It will be slightly different from the form parents use, but the essentials are the same.

"Nicholas! Don't shoot spitballs in this class. I don't like it." Then touch him slightly on the shoulder and say, "I understand you get bored when you don't understand the problem. Tell me when you don't get it. I enjoy helping you."[1]

---

[1] "Touching" students is a sensitive subject these days and may even be against policy in some school systems. Physical contact and touching is important in human interactions, but it may be inappropriate and even risky for a teacher in many cases. The teacher must use his/her best judgment in each case.

Simply put, you form an attachment, and enhance and facilitate learning. You yourself will have to endure the pain of loss each spring as your students move on. But you have made a great impact, giving a lasting gift to a youngster when you are willing to be understanding and helpful in a real way by being truly present and not rejecting.

Q: My ten-year-old is very independent and rarely asks for my help. He is really quite grown-up and makes his own decisions most of the time. I can't imagine giving him a One-Minute Scolding because it would feel like I'm disciplining another adult.

A: Your child pays a heavy price for an "independence" that appears to be so healthy and adult. Actually he is learning not to trust you to be present and helpful for him when he is in need. If he does not learn to trust you and turn to you for help, perceiving you as a loving parent, who can he trust? Such independent children usually grow up to be independent but also lonely and alienated adults who are unable to be intimate and trusting with anyone, including their spouses.

Such children are often born with an "independent" temperament and require unusual strength, consistency, and most important, intensity from their parents. These children require a prompt and intense Scolding for each misdeed. Your expression of positive feelings must be very intense and physical so that your child can *feel* your love.

The degree of "independence" that you describe does not sound like a genuine independence at all, but more like a withdrawal or alienation. Indeed, we raise our children carefully and lovingly with their ultimate independence from us a goal. They love to say, "Let me try it—let me do it all alone." Healthy children very naturally strive for autonomy.

But it is a child's right to find healthy comfort as he proceeds in his development. It is not natural or healthy for a child to turn only to himself for solution to problems. If a youngster turns inward and rarely reaches out for help or direction, especially when he is in trouble, it may mean that either (1) a loving, helpful, consistently present adult has not been available to him, or the adults he knows are too punitive to be trusted for help, or they may be too weak, or (2) the child may have been born with a "hard to reach" temperament.

Either of these conditions causes the youngster to withdraw into himself because he cannot or he will not trust that there is anybody out there who can really help in any way. Such lack of trust only causes intense loneliness and an inability to admit anyone into his real life. Eventually, if not corrected, it can lead to an inability to trust even a spouse— an inability to share, to love, to feel, and to be vulnerable to others. He only feels an alienation and separation from life that allows him to indeed "fend for himself," but that is not the same as independence or autonomy.

Children with an "independent" temperament or orientation require unusual intensity of feeling from their parents. They need strong, consistent, and prompt input for misdeeds. Most important, the expression of positive feelings must also be very intense, penetrating, and even tangible. This is the only way to cure them of their distance and teach them trust. They must know that there really is someone who loves them unconditionally and helps them know right from wrong.

Q: **My eight-year-old child lies all the time. He lies even when it isn't necessary for his protection. Will the One-Minute Scolding help him get over this habit?**

A: When children lie, parents get very upset and fear that this is an indication of a serious flaw of character. A child learns to lie when he feels he cannot trust his parents with the truth. Telling the truth only causes more trouble than he is already in and with no promise of a helpful or compassionate solution.

So when a child has misbehaved and you have very clear evidence of the problem, approach him in a way that shows him clearly that you are there to work this out and help him to a better solution. Do not put him on the spot by asking him questions that will give him a chance to lie and compromise and compound the problem. If you already know the answer, take it from there.

Asking David if he ate the chocolate candy when his face is already decorated with evidence is daring him to lie. Discipline him promptly with the One-Minute Scolding. If it turns out that you have made a mistake and it was only gravy on his chin, apologize sincerely and ask for forgiveness. It gives him a great feeling of being morally in the right for once.

Every chance you get, praise him warmly and intensely whenever he tells the truth. Define him as an honest child in every way you can—even in front of others. If he lies and doesn't live up to that definition of honesty, respond with your surprise and disappointment and then give him a One-Minute Scolding. During the first half of the Scolding state clearly your sorrow that he forgot you were going to help him and that he must trust you with the truth and have faith in your ability to handle the truth. In the positive half of the Scolding, assure him that you'll always help him and that telling the truth makes it easier for you to help him. Promise that you'll discipline him every time until he remembers not to lie, and that you will only scold him and not lose control around him. Tell him that you love him very much and you know that he is a good fellow who really wants to be truthful.

Q: What should I do when I feel like I hate my child?

A: Hate is an extreme form of anger. Parents, all parents, get very angry at their children at different times and for different reasons. It is never helpful to tell your child that you hate him because it implies that there's something wrong with his very being. This usually occurs when problems have gone on for some time and you have been frustrated in trying to get your child to behave more appropriately. The One-Minute Scolding is a tool that will help you get back on the track.

Using the One-Minute Scolding every time your child misbehaves allows you to discharge your anger and frustration rather than letting it build up, and it also helps you to express those warm and loving feelings that most, if not all, parents feel for their children. The first few days or even weeks may require ten or fifteen minutes a day. Don't be discouraged. All parents feel overwhelmed with fear that they are not good parents. After using the Scolding for a period of time, you will find that the number of Scoldings required drops off sharply, and that your child's behavior changes dramatically.

Q: My neighbor has real problems disciplining her children. In fact, I classify her as an abusing parent. Would the One-Minute Scolding be helpful to her?

A: Abusing parents feel helpless in dealing with their lives as well as disciplining their children effectively and in a warm and loving manner. Your support and encouragement could be very helpful to her and her family. If you could develop a relationship with her so that she sees you as a helpful and wise neighbor, she might allow you to teach her how to use the One-Minute Scolding.

Obviously the One-Minute Scolding leads to much happier results than physical and emotional abuse. In my experience, abusing parents have learned to use the One-Minute Scolding very quickly when they have not felt criticized and humiliated and embarrassed because of their troubles in disciplining their children. They are often very grateful and gratified by the results that come shortly after using the One-Minute Scolding.

Q: Can't this method of discipline be misused? Can't you batter children emotionally with the scolding half of the Scolding?

A: Any tool can be misused. The One-Minute Scolding is difficult to misuse if it is carried out properly. Parents find it impossible to continue screaming at their children after they have expressed their warmth and caring in a loving manner in the second half of the Scolding. The Scolding is not just for children. It is designed specifically to help parents be effective, loving parents.

Our problem has been to convince parents to begin using the Scolding and to use it correctly. It has been our experience that parents who use the One-Minute Scolding never batter their children emotionally or psychologically.

Q: I have three or four foster children in my home at one time. I also have a son of my own. These foster children come and go all the time, visiting their mothers, returning, going to live with their father, etc. I notice that just before and just after one of these weekends away, they really get naughty. Should I use the

One-Minute Scolding with these children? Should I try to develop a relationship with these children? Should I use the One-Minute Scolding on my own child as well?

A: Foster parents have used the One-Minute Scolding with remarkable success. When they are encouraged to develop a warm intense relationship with their foster children, even though the children may be living with them for just a few weeks, foster parents can help them thrive by teaching them how to behave, and teaching them values to live by. The One-Minute Scolding has proven to be invaluable to foster parents.

It is easy to use the One-Minute Scolding on your own child as well as your foster children. The tactic is so simple and easy to use that it comes naturally after a few months of regular use. Your foster children will feel cared for as though they were your own, and your own natural son will feel that he's fairly treated and not neglected by your attention to your foster children.

Q: **I'm divorced. When my daughters go to their dad and stepmother's for the summer they live by different rules, and they live a very different lifestyle. What's the use of doing the One-Minute Scolding, setting reasonable limits, and expecting them to behave properly when they get to do anything they want when they live with their father and stepmother?**

A: This is a common problem and often a difficult one to resolve perfectly. However, you have your daughters most of the year, and since discipline is teaching, there's no reason whatsoever why you should feel you cannot teach your children proper behavior and the values that go with them while they live with you.

Children love to know how to behave and what values to live by. They will love you for disciplining them in a consistent and caring manner, and despite their summers in an unstructured, unsupervised situation, nothing can take that from them. Children who are unsupervised and uncared for are sad, lonely, and angry kids. Perhaps if you approach your ex-husband in a positive and friendly manner he will cooperate in setting appropriate limits and disciplining them in a consistent manner.

Q: My two-year-old bites when he's angry, and my mom told me that if we bite him back he'll learn fast what that feels like. Frankly, I can't imagine just talking about it would get through to him. Will the Scolding work for my two-year-old?

A: Biting your two-year-old hard enough to make him stop usually causes fear and mistrust in your child. As you know, a bite hurts a lot. Use the One-Minute Scolding instead. A two-year-old needs only a very short first half of the Scolding, but it should be sharp and intense in response to his biting. A dramatic, loud "no" when he bites followed by reassuring warmth immediately afterwards will soon teach him not to bite. Try it for a few days. You will be delightfully surprised.

Q: Recently I saw my son misbehave while playing with his friends outside. I called him in to give him the One-Minute Scolding in private. But he became terribly upset with me because I wasn't going to let him explain and I ended up not scolding him, but sending him to his room. How should I have handled that?

A: Remember that discipline is teaching. If your son was so upset because of what had happened outside or because you had called him in from his play with his friends, he is not "ready" to be taught. Encourage him to express his anger, frustration, and resentment until he is ready to listen. This may take a few hours if he has learned that screaming and yelling at you will get him his way. However, if you will persist, remaining calm and responsive, he will eventually calm down and can be disciplined.

Then proceed with the Scolding, first reassuring him that it will take only a minute and that he can go out to play after you have finished the discipline. If he continues to protest, hear him out and then ask him if he is ready for his One-Minute Scolding. Obviously, he will be anxious to return to his play outside and will soon learn that if he "takes his medicine," and it only takes a minute, he will then be free to return to his play.

Q: When I get angry and scold my boy and then right away hug him and praise him and tell him how much I love him, I feel like I'm pushing his feelings around. Isn't this confusing to a child?

A: At first it is. But after you have done it a few times he will come to expect and appreciate your disciplinary efforts. Your boy knows that you can be angry with him and also love him at the same time. Expressing those feelings, first anger and then abruptly switching to love and care, is a very effective way to teach him how to handle two strong conflicting feelings at the same time.

Chapter 13

A Rapid Review

This chapter is a rapid review of the One-Minute Scolding. Making major changes in your thinking is never easy. Breaking old habits takes time. The way you were scolded as a child, and probably the way you've tried to discipline your own up until this frustrating point has been a part of you for years. So be patient with yourself as you change your punishments of the past into this better disciplinary technique, the One-Minute Scolding.

To help yourself make the changes you want and to get the results more quickly, this chapter was prepared as a quick review. Read it or scan it daily for the first month. You'll be pleased and surprised at how quickly you will be able to master the technique.

Before I Begin the Scolding

The One-Minute Scolding is discipline, not a discussion.

I am the only one allowed to talk during the Scolding. I will remind my child that he is being disciplined and that he may talk with me after the Scolding.

The One-Minute Scolding is painful for my child.

He will try whatever it takes to get me to stop. He may laugh, look bored, interrupt, squirm away, or try a variety of other maneuvers to get me to stop using the One-Minute Scolding. But I love my child enough to continue to use the One-Minute Scolding until he learns to behave himself and, in the process, to like himself.

No matter what happens, I complete the Scolding.

For the One-Minute Scolding to be effective, I must do the entire disciplinary act, regardless of circumstances. I will allow nothing to interfere with completing this process which is so important for my child's well-being.

I will assess my anger.

Before I begin the One-Minute Scolding, I must assess the amount of anger that I have inside. Angry feelings must match the misbehavior and not other events of the day.

The First Half of the Scolding

I scold my child in private.

I do this because I do not want to humiliate my child in front of others and because I know that when my child and I are alone together, he is better able to concentrate on his misbehavior and how it affects our relationship.

I make physical contact with my child.

Depending upon my child's age, I put him on my lap, or I put my arm around his shoulder, or I hold onto his forearm, or I at least have my fingertips on his shirt sleeves.

I stay in physical contact with my child for the next minute.

My hands, face, and body communicate first my angry and disappointed feelings and then my warm and caring feelings directly to my child. He cannot "turn off" or hide from that communication.

I express my feelings in simple and clear language.

My child must understand the rule he has broken. So, I describe clearly the misbehavior or the broken rule that caused my anger. For example, "I am angry because you did X, Y, and Z. I get very angry when you do that."

I express how angry or upset I am.

I want my child to learn to understand and express feelings. I say, "I am so angry that I want to spank you." In this way, I am teaching my child *how* to deal with strong feelings and, by example, *how not* to deal with strong feelings, such as hitting, retreating, or feeling hurt.

I communicate my feelings with my body language, tone of voice, and facial expression, as well as with the words that I use.

My words, body language, and facial expressions must all be congruous and thus not confuse my child as to the message being sent. Otherwise, I will not be effectively teaching my child the good behavior I want her to learn.

I continue to express my feelings about my child's behavior until I see that my child feels my anger or disappointment.

I will know this is accomplished when I see a change in mood (tears, facial expressions, trembling lip, etc.). My child feels that this misbehavior has upset me. She, too, is in a state of excitability. This tells me the first half of the Scolding is over.

I keep my scolding brief.

I realize that I may have a great deal of unexpressed anger that I would like to vent. However, I know that if I prolong the first half of the Scolding or make it too intense, my child can "tune out" or get too worried and not learn what I want to teach. I do not try to get all of my feelings out in one One-Minute Scolding.

The Second Half of the Scolding

I take a few deep breaths and remind myself how important my child is to me.

I have my child's full attention. Now, I want him to be flooded with my warmth and caring.

I abruptly change to a tone of voice, facial expression, and body language that is warm and caring.

I have told my child what I am angry about, how angry and upset I am, and now I must communicate my love and concern for my child in a clear and consistent manner. This rewards the child for listening.

I express my love and concern for my child.

Again, I use simple language. "You are a good boy. I know you want to behave. I want to be a good parent, and I'm going to help you." My tone of voice, my touch, and my facial expression all must be consistent with the words that I use.

I validate my child as a person of importance and integrity.

I tell her that she is a good person. I tell her that I want her to grow up to be a good, strong, healthy woman. I tell her that she's a person of value.

I remind my child that when she misbehaves, I discipline her.

I tell her, "I am disciplining you because you misbehaved. I care for you so much that I am going to discipline you every time you make a mistake like that." I tell her that if she breaks the rule again, I will discipline her again.

I tell my child that it is easy to discipline him.

Discipline need not be a hardship nor something to be avoided. I love my child. I discipline my child because I love him. I want my child to feel certain strength and maturity. My child will be relieved if I can discipline him in a simple, effective, and consistent manner.

I reassure my child that whenever she breaks a rule and needs discipline, I will be there to give her the discipline she needs.

"Every time you blow it, I'm going to discipline you because I love you. It's no big deal for me. I like to be a good, strong parent. So I'll discipline you every time you make a mistake. It's easy for me."

The Conclusion of the Scolding

Did my child learn what I wanted him to learn?

I want to be effective. I want to know if my child learned the lesson of the moment. So I ask, "Why am I disciplining you now?" I wait for an answer. If he doesn't know, it means that either he doesn't want to tell me, or that the scolding half of the Scolding has been too vigorous and his fear and anxiety have flooded him and interfered with the learning of that which I wanted to teach. So I tell him, "I'm disciplining you because you hit your sister."

I ask him why I discipline him every time he misbehaves.

"Now, why do I discipline you every time you blow it?" I want him to respond with, "Because you love me." If he doesn't recall, I tell him again, "I love you." Or, if I find it difficult to express such intense positive feelings for my child at the time, I may say, "I care for you very much."

I end a One-Minute Scolding by hugging or touching my child.

The hug tells him that I love him and discipline is over. An older adolescent may only allow me to pat him on the shoulder or on the arm. This sign of affection is the signal that I have finished the discipline.

After I have disciplined my child, I let it go.

When the Scolding is over, it's over! I do not mention it again. I do not ask my spouse to discipline him for a second time.

We may want to discuss the matter, but there will be no more Scoldings for the misbehavior that just occurred. One Scolding per act of wrongdoing is enough.

I encourage my child to do whatever she wishes after the One-Minute Scolding.

My child may choose to stay near me or to go off by herself to think about things.

I encourage my child to express her feelings at this time.

My child may be angry or sad and may want to talk about her feelings. I encourage her and listen patiently. She may tell me that she doesn't think that the Scolding was fair. She may tell me that she is angry and upset with me for disciplining her. I listen to her carefully. I hear her out and, unless I am proved wrong later, I do not apologize, nor do I make excuses for disciplining her. I disciplined her because I love her.

She may not want to talk about her feelings immediately, but she may want to do so later. This I should support and encourage.

Again, What Are the Five Steps of the One-Minute Scolding?

1. Scolding the behavior
2. A moment of transition
3. Positive reaffirmation of the child's worth
4. A short quiz of the rules
5. Affectionate physical contact

Always remember, the One-Minute Scolding is discipline that teaches. It is not punishment.

PART III

Beyond the One-Minute Scolding— Problems That Require Professional Help

Chapter 14

Help for Unattached or "Numb" Children

This chapter will outline the dynamics that can occur when a child is unattached to his parents and the response of the family to his misbehaviors. Most children are attached to their parents in some degree or another, but a large and increasing number of children are truly unattached to any adult caretaker. If you have ever wondered why your child, or another child, seems distant and unattached to his parents, this chapter will provide a common sense understanding of how the child becomes unattached, his many behaviors that signal attempts to achieve an attachment, and the parent's responses to these behaviors. In addition, if you know of a child in your neighborhood or in your extended family who shows signs of being emotionally detached from others, you will be able to better understand why, and possibly steer the youngster and his family toward understanding and treatment.

This chapter also provides additional understanding of the bonding process between parent and child. We will also discuss some of the more common psychological and emotional

responses of the unattached child and his family and some strategies of the therapist who tries to help parent or caretaker and child
develop a trusting relationship. We will describe methods that may
minimize the adverse effects of the child's losses and fears of abandonment and lay the foundation for future mental health.

The Biological Roots of Attachment

As we discussed in Chapter 7, baby mammals are helpless and
dependent on their mothers for sustenance and protection. They
die if their mother does not provide constant care and food. They
survive to adulthood if their mothers and family provide an adequate, nurturing, and protected environment. Baby mammals
have behaviors that cause their mothers to form bonds or attachments to them, and this process is mediated by feelings. The baby
feels distress and need, and behaves in a way that causes the
mother to feel aroused, and therefore, moved to action. These
maternal actions tend to restore the baby to a peaceful feeling
state, one of low arousal. The baby's attachment feelings and
behaviors are reinforced by mother's caretaking responses.

This attachment process is vital to the survival of the individual mammal to adulthood, and therefore, for the preservation
of the species.

Human Infants and Bonding

Human babies are very helpless and vulnerable, requiring almost
constant attention and care for many years. Often, they must be
cared for by mothers who may have other children requiring care.
This feat demands a high level of organization by the mother, and
she must both face and respond to the baby's many complex feeling
states. Also, some children are difficult to nurture, and consequently, they provide few rewards to the caring, responsive mother.

The newborn infant is totally dependent upon his human environment for survival. An infant will quickly succumb if not protected, cared for, and nurtured. The bond he develops with his mother is vital if he is to survive. He has depended on her milk and her close attention and fierce protection as many other infants have for thousands of years.

The anger and rage expressed when the infant is in need arises from a sense of survival being threatened. If the infant is not fed or cared for, he will respond with intense feelings, terror and rage (high arousal), until a caretaker meets his basic needs of food, warmth, and comforting. When a parent comforts a child or meets the child's needs, the child's high level of arousal is lowered to a more relaxed state.

This arousal-relaxation cycle builds trust in the child. The mother is also placed in a high state of arousal when she experiences the child crying. The mother's arousal is relieved when the child stops crying. This interaction between infant and mother, or any adult who routinely comforts or meets the physical and emotional needs of a child, causes the child and the mother to form feeling bonds or an attachment. (For the sake of convenience, I will use "mother" as a synonym for any nurturing caretaker and usually identify the child as a boy with the understanding that both boys and girls may have an attachment problem.)

The Mother-Infant Bond

Exactly how this bonding process occurs between mother and infant is not fully understood, but some explanations are more plausible, as well as useful.

The mother responds appropriately to the child's needs, causing the child to feel good. If the child is hungry, feels "bad" (high arousal), the mother feeds the child and the child feels good. The child soon comes to learn that his mama is a person who consistently makes him feel good. The child's cries cause Mama to feel bad or distressed (high arousal). Mama feeds the child, the child stops crying, and then Mama feels good (arousal is lowered). The child becomes a source of pleasure for the mother. The mother is a source of pleasure for the child. This interaction between infant and mother causes them both to feel good, and they soon come to like or love that person who makes them feel good.

There is nothing mysterious about this process. The common-sense theory we use is that bonding or attachment occurs between parent and child if their interaction consistently gives the other pleasure. A helpless, vulnerable infant feels pleasure when fed or when his diaper is changed because his distress is eased. When the child's mother consistently and repetitively cares for the child, the child soon learns to expect pleasure or lowering of arousal from that mother.

The repeated, comforting care by the mother consists of many caretaking behaviors that meet the child's needs and therefore enhance attachment. This "mother-care" lowers arousal and takes on a tension-relieving quality. These caretaking behaviors also include: touching, eye contact, soft and high-pitched to low-pitched speech, and movement while holding (rocking).

All of these caretaking behaviors will lower arousal and therefore will be associated with a good feeling in the infant. He will come to like these behaviors of his mother, so long as they are associated with a good feeling.

The Emotional Life of the Child

Many believe, myself included, that infants and children have a great capacity for feelings. They do not have the cognitive development to distinguish complex feelings (e.g., such as differentiating jealousy from resentment), but they do have the capacity to be enraged or terrified, as well as delighted or joyful.

Most adults have seen and heard small children wail and express great distress when lost or separated from their caretaker in a strange and alien environment such as a large market. The cries of the terrified lost child can touch anyone's heart.

Most of us have also observed small children playing peek-a-boo, and we enjoy their obvious delight. This ability to feel has a survival value. The small infant has the tools to elicit intense feelings in a caretaker so that the caretaker will not abandon him. The child can engage the feelings of an adult in such a way so that the adult will "fall in love" with the child, and therefore keep the adult around permanently.

The small child is by nature a sensitive being who responds to frightening or painful experiences with fear. Most small children turn to someone in their family who consistently provides relief from that pain by quieting the arousal, relieving the fear, and comforting the hurt. That person is usually the mother, but frequently it can be the father, sibling, or other relative. Anyone would suffice, so long as it is someone who will be consistently protective and nurturing.

If mother/caretaker is not readily available to the child when in distress, the child must deal with his feelings alone. The baby, without a secure attachment to his mother, feels constantly distressed. He behaves in a way that should engage a nurturing caretaker. This behavior is termed "attachment behavior," and includes crying, whining, clinging, or any behavior that causes his caretaker to focus her attention onto him. Attention-seeking behavior is often attachment behavior. Behavior that consistently "pushes Mama's buttons" is nearly always attachment behavior. The caretaking behaviors of the parent usually lower the arousal of the child. This is pleasurable for the child, and therefore facilitates bonding.

A lost two-year-old wailing for his mother in a large shopping mall causes all but the most hard-hearted to respond with distress. Few of us could casually walk past that terrified child, indifferent to his or her plight. This arousal, this feeling response to the lost child, is a natural feeling that powerfully motivates us to do something to relieve that child and stop that painful wailing. This child is signaling to us; he is communicating his feelings of intense distress and panic to us in such a way that we are almost stopped in our tracks with the responsive feeling of wanting to care for that child. These feeling states between panicked child and observers continue until the child is restored to his caretaker and stops wailing. The onlooker may then proceed with his tasks, and usually promptly forgets the entire event. This is a clear demonstration of attachment behavior. The child was lost, felt panic and terror, called for his mama, and was comforted when reunited with her.

From Attachment to Independence

As a child grows and achieves some measure of autonomy and mobility, the development of fine and gross motor skills and speech allows the child to interact with and manipulate the environment to meet his needs. He is no longer totally dependent on his parents to meet his needs. Dangers and social expectations require the parents to set limits on their child's actions. In the normally attached child, a healthy autonomy begins to develop. The child makes choices within reasonable limits set by his parents. If the parents respond in a healthy way to their child's normal curiosity and need to explore the environment, the child develops a "win-win" view of human relationships. The child learns to trust that Mom and Dad frustrate him for his own protection and well-being.

When a child is frustrated by limits, he usually develops a state of arousal. He will always try to communicate his distress to his trusted parents. If they lower his arousal and yet firmly expect compliance to their limits and wishes, the child will learn to tolerate frustration and abide by his parents' limits. As parents comfort their child when he is frustrated or distressed, they reinforce or encourage appropriate behavior. They are teaching him how to behave, despite feeling anxious, angry, or fearful. Smiles, praise, cuddling, play interaction, distractions, and soothing all lower arousal, comfort the child, distract him from his forbidden activity and reward him for compliance with the parent's wishes.

When a child comes to associate a certain feeling with a specific behavior, he is developing a conscience. Conscience is learned primarily from the parent's feeling response to the child's behaviors. When he pokes a metal object into an electric outlet and his mother reacts with intense fear, he quickly learns to associate the electric outlet with fear because he feels his mother's emotional response, and he remembers it. Or, if a child runs out into a busy street and his father grabs him and gives the child an immediate and very intense scolding, the child soon learns to associate crossing that street with his father's feelings. If the parental feeling response is consistently repeated whenever the child misbehaves, the child learns to associate a specific feeling with a specific behavior.

Obviously, the child should also be rewarded for good and appropriate behavior so that the child quickly learns what is desired behavior. Much of what the child learns is by modeling after the parents, but the parents can also teach a great deal by careful attention to their feeling responses to the child's behavior. Certain children respond much more quickly to consistent, intense positive parental responses and tend to resist and actively oppose negative reinforcement, such as painful punishment.

"Doing good" feels good! "Doing bad" feels bad!

The Roots of Unattachment

There are many difficulties and problems that befall any mother and her infant. These troubles and conflicts are resolved relatively easily if the pair have a long, intense, mutually satisfying relationship. If mother and child inflict painful wounds on each other as they interact, both will find life easier if they avoid each other.

What if there is no one to whom the child can turn to for comfort? What if mother or caretaker reacts with hostility, indifference, anger, or helplessness to the child's attachment behaviors? Such children stay aroused, fearful, anxious, terrified, and panicky until the fearful situation disappears or until the child has "numbed out" his terror and no longer feels or responds to the feared stimuli with anxiety or fear. The sensitive, curious, vulnerable, learning child stops feeling. He no longer feels the feelings of others, especially the less intense, more subtle feelings of others. He loses the capacity of empathy and sometimes this loss is permanent.

A child who does not have a secure, unconflicted attachment to his mother or other caretaker becomes fearful, anxious, numbed out, depressed, and enraged. All these feelings have to be dealt with, consuming energy and time, and consequently learning is hindered and diminished. A child consistently denied maternal care usually develops an emotional and behavioral complex clinically recognized as a syndrome of maternal deprivation. This child is dull and developmentally and emotionally retarded. The child is preoccupied with self-protection; he cannot interact with his environment or develop his many-faceted potential.

If a child is repeatedly placed in a situation that reminds him of previously painful experiences, the child naturally feels fear or anxiety. An anxious or fearful child spends more time tending to his defenses than to his environment. Then the child stops learning, and curiosity is diminished. More distressing, the child learns to turn away from people and his environment to protect himself from danger. A child who does not have a parent or caretaker consistently available for him when he is in need is a child who is going to be in a chronic state of high arousal. This is a dangerous psychological state for a child and will be discussed in detail later in this chapter.

When the Attachment Process Fails

If parents are uncomfortable with their child's expression of anger and frustration, and are unable to comfort the child while maintaining the limits and values they have established, the attachment process often goes awry. The child and his parents probably will then develop a deviant or weak bond or attachment. When the attachment process goes awry, the child's emotional and psychological development is significantly affected, and he may demonstrate signs and symptoms of psychopathology (inappropriate, deviant, and difficult behaviors and feelings).

The child may learn how to get his way regardless of his parent's limits and wishes, or he may hide his arousal and not go to his parents for comfort. He may escape into fantasy, he may complain of physical symptoms such as frequent belly-aches, he may become depressed, or he could even become psychotic (see or hear things others do not see or hear). The nature of his maladaptive response depends on his basic temperament and his innate mental toughness. The basic problem is that the parents are unable to consistently and appropriately comfort or lower the child's arousal. The ability to perceive the child's discomfort and respond appropriately is the primary parental task and is essential for attachment to proceed normally.

The Cost of an Insecure Attachment

A secure attachment is absolutely essential for the normal development and even the survival of the child. The child's extraordinarily long dependent period is essential for normal language and social development. This prolonged period of secure dependency is the base upon which he matures into a healthy adult, capable of forming complex relationships and performing high-level cognitive operations. The failure of the attachment process to effect a secure bond to an adult caretaker threatens this extremely important process.

The young child's affective (feeling) response to separation from his parents is usually intense whether obvious or not, and the loss of a trusted parent is always extreme. While often covert and "defended," the rage/terror reaction to loss is always intense because it represents the primitive rage and fear of the infant—a matter of survival. The covert, hidden, and defended quality of a rage/terror reaction is probably caused by an intense conflict within the child. If a child's very security is threatened, his affective response is very high arousal (terror or rage). He discharges his feelings by screaming or similar behaviors. As an attachment message or communication to his parents, it should cause a normal, healthy caretaker to respond appropriately with care and nurturing, which comforts the child and lowers his arousal.

However, if the parent is consistently absent, indifferent, or hostile in response to the child's attachment behaviors, the child must adapt to survive. The child's response may be to conserve psychic energy and become depressed. His physiological and psychological mechanisms slow down; thus, depression becomes an adaptive response to an intolerable situation. Or, the child may develop somatic symptoms that bring about caring and nurturing. Asthmatic symptoms, eczema, belly-aches, headaches, and other psychosomatic symptoms are a common response to attachment problems probably because the parent has responded to the child's complaints with care. If the stress is intolerable, prolonged or intense, the child could even become psychotic (the child is unable to maintain a separation between the outer world and the inner psychic world of feelings, thoughts, dreams, and fantasies). These signs and symptoms may be the manifestation of a unsuccessful attachment.

Attachment Needs and Behavior

However, even the most damaged child, numbed out and developmentally behind, continues to seek an attachment to available caretakers. All children seem to have a unique ability to put their parents in a high state of arousal. These behaviors cause the parent to focus immediately on the child with intense feelings and narrow focus. A child has many opportunities to learn just which of his many behaviors can elicit intense responses from his parents. Parents with tender ears find their children using four letter words whenever the child needs immediate attention. Mothers who value a neat, clean house have children who inevitably mess up the house whenever necessary. Children with constant high levels of anxiety, fears, or sadness will tend to continuously seek their parent's help in lowering these uncomfortable feelings.

Parents may "give up" after failing in their efforts to comfort their child, leaving both parent and child frustrated and angry. Often children who have lost a parent through divorce or separation fear that the remaining parent will also leave. This child tends to be anxious, fearful, and sad because painful events have frightened him; he fears another loss. Children with tense, withdrawn, and preoccupied parents remain unconsoled when frightened because their parents are unavailable or cannot comfort them.

If a child is genetically strong and temperamentally demanding of a bond with a parent, he or she can compel the parent to respond and form an attachment. If the parent persists and demands a relationship with a temperamentally insensitive child, a bond can also form. If both parent and child are too weak or too resistant and insecure, an unstable, ambivalent attachment forms and the child continues to exhibit frequent and intense attachment behaviors. This puts the parent in a continued high state of arousal, a discomfort that will persist until the pair find a way to lower their arousal and bond, or until the child gives up and "numbs out."

Small children seek the proximity of their caretakers when frightened or aroused. The physical presence of a parent nearby is often all that is necessary to restore the child to a peaceful state. If the child seeks his parent for comfort, and his parent responds with anger, rejection, or disapproval, the child is not only not relieved of his painful feeling state, but he learns to be wary and even afraid of his parent. He then tends not to seek their help when troubled or upset. He turns to himself or perhaps to his peers. A parent who abuses his child, verbally or physically, teaches his child to be afraid of him.

A child does not use only clinging, whining, temper tantrums, or wails of terror to engage the attention of his parents. He uses a wide range of attachment behaviors that proceed from a myriad of feelings, wants, and goals. Not only must his parents be perceptive and knowledgeable regarding his needs and developmental goals, but above all, they must be empathic to his feeling states. Children do not have the ability to verbalize their problems and their feelings accurately. Their parents must be sensitive to their feelings and what may be causing them. This is often a difficult task, and in our culture is becoming more so because so many of our children are being raised in single-parent homes with an exhausted, overwhelmed parent and no extended family available for support and assistance.

The Roots of "Numbing Out"

"Numbing out," is the most alarming and most common response to the profound failure of the attachment process. It is probably inevitable if there is repeated loss of attachment figures, but it also may occur if there is only one serious loss of a parent.

Numbing may be a self-protective physiological device. A child can maintain a high state of arousal only for a limited time because he has limited endurance and strength. There must be a psychophysiologic mechanism that causes the child to stop responding to the lack of care with terror or rage; the child's body cannot sustain it. The limbic system, a part of the brain which handles feelings, has a mechanism that causes the individual to stop responding to the lack of care with such high levels of arousal. This diminished responsiveness to stress is the basis of numbing out.

Children tend to use primitive and immature ego-defense mechanisms to cope with prolonged and intensive negative feelings. Abandoned, unattached kids tend to numb out their feelings of terror, rage, and sadness that would normally be used to engage the attention of the caretaker. If these feelings fall upon deaf or inattentive ears, or bring anger, resentment, or fear from the caretaker, this will increase the distress of the child. Children will try repeatedly to seek an attachment to a fear-reducing caretaker, but if these attachment efforts fail, the child will ultimately turn to himself for relief. Numbing out his feelings allows the child some comfort, but it also significantly interferes with the child's ability to "hear" or feel the feelings of others.

I have spoken to a number of numbed-out adults who recall the exact moment when, as children, they decided that they must care for themselves and not expect any help from their parents. They recall, with intense emotion, the feelings of alienation (an intense feeling of loneliness and sense that one does not belong to any group) and sadness that replaced their fear and anger. They understood their situation and accepted it usually without bitter ill will towards their unaware parents.

Unconsciously, these children began to manipulate and control their parents to meet their dependency needs. We have all seen children like this—little dictators, subtly or overtly running the family much to everyone's distress. So unattached children are not only "numbed out," they are also consistently manipulative, controlling, and usually lie, cheat, steal, and often become defiant and oppositional.

When these children enter school, they use these same mechanisms on their teachers and other adults. Unless the teacher is comfortably able to control such a numbed-out, manipulative child, the teaching process is frustrated and the child and his classmates do not learn. We find an increasing percentage of children of this kind in the classroom, and usually a frustrated, angry teacher is spending most of her time teaching her children how to behave in the classroom, rather than the academic subjects she expected to teach. As one might predict, these numbed-out, unattached children have problems learning.

Numbed-out children are insensitive to the feelings of others. They have little or no empathy for others. Their focus of attention is on themselves. They have no inclination or need to be attentive to others because they have learned there is no help from others. This lack of empathy, this insensitivity to the feelings of others, leads to profound difficulty in trusting, and therefore they are unable to form an intimate relationship to others. These children do not develop an adequate conscience. They do not feel anxiety when contemplating an antisocial act and feel no guilt or remorse afterwards.

Characteristics of Numbing Out

Loss of Trust

A common adaptive response for a child who cannot achieve a trusting attachment is for the child to parent himself, assuming responsibility for meeting his own needs. He does not expect to get comfort or the lowering of arousal from his caretakers, so he takes care of himself. He might, for example, not even alert his parents that he is suicidal. He does not trust others—he trusts only himself.

Resistance and Distance

The child resists closeness, because if he feels cared for by others, he could be abandoned, and this is an intolerable fear. Numbed-out children fiercely insist on emotional distance, resisting comforting by caretakers. They will not allow their caretakers to rock them and comfort them. Some of these children, especially those who have been sexually abused or maternally deprived, will paradoxically be bottomless pits for affection, never seeming to get enough. These children are numbed out and distant, unable to feel the caring expressed by the caretaker. Their insatiable demands for affection soon cause their caretakers to avoid these children.

Control

The numbed-out child tends to be extremely controlling, often overtly, but also very subtly and effectively. Caretakers usually respond to the child's controlling behaviors in a variety of ways, but unless they are very strong and confident, they often fail in their efforts to regain control over the child.

Manipulation

Manipulation of others and the environment is but another manifestation of control. The child does not trust others to meet his needs, so he manipulates his environment to do so. We call this "manipulative dependency," which is characteristic of children who have numbed out in response to the failure of the attachment process.

Reversal of Behavioral Learning Pattern

The normal attachment responses lose their reinforcing quality. The child, now desiring distance from others and resistant to control, seeks to keep distance and to minimize the demands and expectations of others. Behaviors that drive people away or lessen their demands are thus reinforced. The reinforcement of negative behaviors leads to a "learned pathology." A child who has experienced multiple abandonments and has been placed in several different foster homes will behave as though he wants to be abandoned once he has settled down. He is testing the human environment to determine whether he will once again be abandoned.

Feeling and Cognitive Responses

Numbed-out children feel intense sadness and loneliness because they cannot feel the feelings of others. They also characteristically feel alienated, that is, they do not feel they belong to anyone, any family, or any social group. They tend to feel unworthy, having poor self-worth or poor self-esteem. They feel they are not worthwhile enough to be cared for or deserving of affection. Frequently, these children are confused. Their cognitive function is adversely affected by the intense feelings of anger, fear, and sadness. They have difficulty thinking in general and especially when upset. They often do not know what they feel. They may express anger when they are feeling fear or sadness. This makes it difficult for others to respond appropriately to the child's feelings.

The Permanent Cost of "Numbing Out"

There is evidence to suggest that if high arousal and the numbing-out response continues long enough, the numbing out becomes permanent. The child is now handicapped by his inability to feel the feelings of others. He is now similar to the child who is genetically insensitive to others. Numbing out causes the child not to care because he does not feel the feelings of others. This defense causes enormous problems for the child, his caretakers, and teachers. He is very difficult to teach. He tends to be relatively unresponsive to the efforts of others to get his attention and learn new information unless the attention-value of the others or the lesson is quite high.

The "Numbed-Out" Adult

The end state of development for the numbed-out child is a seriously emotionally and psychologically impaired adult. These adults feel empty, lonely, and alienated. They do not feel they belong to any group or family. They tend to seek out excitement constantly by driving recklessly, aggressively looking for a fight, seeking exciting sexual partners, gambling, and using drugs and alcohol.

The numbed-out child expects authority to be arbitrary and punitive, unreasonable and ineffectual. He says, "you can't make me." As an adult, these individuals are disdainful and disrespectful of authority. They test and challenge authority, and they are repeatedly at odds with bosses and other authority figures. As adults, they have brief, situational relationships. Family and marital relationships are unstable, although they may return to a few individuals repeatedly if these individuals meet their needs. However, there is no loyalty.

The unattached, numbed-out child becomes the adult without a conscience. He is often amoral. For them a crime is what they get caught doing, not what they have done. They are unwilling to abide by values, although most can verbalize an impressive list of moral values.

Their long-term goals are rarely achieved, and short-term goals or impulses prevail. There is little or no awareness of the past or future consequences of their choices. They have damaging lapses of judgment and forethought; they are repeatedly self-defeating, and never foresee predictable stress. They have no regard for long-term consequences.

The numbed-out adult's emotional state ranges from ice-cold indifference and carelessness, to violent, explosive rage. His feeling state can rarely be modified by the feeling state of others. He has learned no internal control or regulation, so he cannot control his behaviors and choices over drinking, drugs, sex, and money.

These individuals are often labeled as sociopaths and may end up in prison. However, many are successful in business and government, using their charm and flexibility to build companies and achieve government positions responsible for large sums of money, but they manipulate and control to meet their seemingly insatiable needs for self-gratification.

As we all know, the treatment for such individual adults is almost impossible. Our best hope is prevention, treating these children early and aggressively, and perhaps establishing programs to identify high-risk children and intervening before the child numbs out.

Treating the Unattached or "Numbed-Out" Child

The treatment for the abandoned and unattached child is to compel him to form a trusting relationship with a caring adult. He must learn to be vulnerable and ask for help. He must learn to attend to the feelings of others and allow their feelings to affect him. Manipulation and control must be immediately and consistently confronted and disallowed. Proper behavior must be taught and insisted upon. Careful monitoring of conscience formation may guide the treatment process.

There are three basic components of a successful treatment strategy:

1. A therapist who knows what the problem is and what must be done to successfully treat the child, and who has the skill and power to do so.
2. Control of the child's environment so that he cannot manipulate and control his need fulfillment in a maladaptive manner.
3. A caring parent-figure who has the intense feelings available for the child and a long-term commitment to the child.

The first component for successful treatment for the unattached, numbed-out, abandoned child is that a therapist must recognize the problem for what it is and know how to fix it. She must have the ability and the power to instruct the family, control the environment, and support and encourage all involved, so that they stay engaged in the long and difficult treatment process.

The second component includes adequate control of the child's environment, especially all significant adults. Everyone must see the problem in a reasonably congruent way. One significant adult who has a need for the child to act out antisocially may sabotage a treatment program.

The third component of a successful treatment strategy must include an informed, competent parent-figure or caretaker willing to expend the intense feelings for the duration necessary for the child to form an attachment to her. Usually, a therapist cannot do this, nor must they be expected to do this. Only a natural parent, foster parent, adoptive parent, stepparent, or a caretaker in a residential treatment facility is able to provide the intense, caring feelings, the long-term commitment, and the many interactions necessary to form a trusting bond.

Some adults working in hospitals and residential treatment facilities, as well as some therapists, have a special ability to form intense, enduring attachments to their young patients. Their success seems to lie in their ability to compel the child to experience their feelings. Some parents and professionals intuitively perceive the needs of the unattached or abandoned child, and therefore are able to provide the necessary remediation. However, as the literature points out, there is a very high incidence of failure with these children both by caretakers and therapists.

Individual therapy for the unattached child is probably not wise. The patient must be the impaired bond that exists between parents and child—not the child alone. Family therapy with and without the child seems most effective in repairing the bonds. The therapist does not have the time nor the appropriate relationship to form the kind of bond that would repair the underlying damage to the child. Individual therapy at a later date may be appropriate.

Preparing the Caregivers

Most parents and caretakers are willing to try to participate in this treatment program, but soon find themselves uncomfortable with the intense and exhausting emotional and psychological demands it makes. We have found it vital to administer the Minnesota Multiphasic Personality Inventory (MMPI) to the caretakers, so that we know how to better help them with this very difficult task.

After the initial diagnostic family session, the parents are given feedback on their MMPI profiles. The information from the testing gives us an avenue to the best way to relate to the parents so they are not alienated or made too anxious as we proceed to help them change their way of bonding to their child. Although the first several family therapy sessions include information gathering, we ask the parents in the first treatment session to change the way they discipline and relate to their child. Most parents and caretakers are willing to begin a treatment program, but soon find themselves uncomfortable and stressed by the intense and exhausting emotional and psychological demands it makes. Knowing their MMPI profiles, which indicates their basic fears, allows the therapist to respond empathically, and therefore appropriately, to the parent's feelings.

The key to the successful treatment of the unattached child lies in the ability of the therapist to form an attachment to the caretakers, so that they "internalize" her messages and use the same empathic understanding of the child as the therapist uses with them. The therapist must feel the hurt, rage, fear, dread, and ambivalence these parents feel. The therapist must encourage the expression of these feelings by the caretakers, and if they are unable to because of fear, their feelings should be demonstrated imaginatively and sympathetically by the therapist so that the parents can begin to discharge their feelings and feel more comfortable doing it. We have found that an intellectual understanding of the dynamics underlying the family problems is most useful when integrated with the expression of feelings that underlie behaviors.

It may take several family sessions before the parents fully understand that underlying their attempts to change the way they are controlling and disciplining their child must be a radical change in their understanding of why they and their child feel and behave the way they do. They must come to understand and empathize with their child so that they can respond in an appropriate and healing manner.

Control and Discipline Techniques

The first two issues we focus on are control and discipline. The parents must be in control, and they must teach their child how to behave, how to relate, and what values to hold, and at the same time, develop a warm, trusting attachment to the parents. Appropriate controlling techniques are taught to the parents; at these times the child will not be present. Some children are so clever and persistent in their efforts to control that parents need every possible advantage.

The "Holding" Technique

I encourage parents to "hold" their children as a way to help them establish dominance. The "hold" is a restraining method in which the parent holds the child on his or her lap firmly, but without pain or physically hurting the child, until the child agrees verbally that "Mom or Dad is the boss." This usually takes a couple of hours of emotional and physical work that leaves both the parent and the child exhausted. It is not recommended for the faint of heart or for parents who cannot physically control the child for two or more hours. Parents are warned that they must be prepared for a grueling work-out. I encourage them to set the time for the first "hold" when they are both ready, and when I am available for telephone consultation, support, and encouragement. The book, *Holding Time: How to Eliminate Conflict, Temper Tantrums, and Sibling Rivalry and Raise Happy, Loving, Successful Children*, by Martha G. Welch, M.D., is also helpful.

The result is often surprising to the parents because they fear that after a two-hour intensely emotional struggle their child will harbor resentment and anger. Nothing is further from the truth; the child is nearly always very happy the next day, feeling relaxed and hopeful that his world will become a safe and secure one in which Mom and Dad can handle the scary outside world as well as the terrors and rages the child feels and fears. (I've included a much more extensive discussion on this "holding" technique in Chapter 15.)

Older children who cannot be physically controlled must be controlled verbally. Parents need to be reminded that they do usually know more than their youngster, and that they do care about their child and want what is best for him. They need to be reminded that everyone benefits if they are in control and are the boss. I teach parents the basics of communication theory so that they can define and redefine the relationship and thus control their child. We role-play and rehearse until parents are comfortable being the boss.

We also encourage parents to read Gregory Bodenhamer's book, *Back in Control: How to Get Your Children to Behave*, and to follow his instructions to the letter. His basic method is to have parents be clear in their minds as to what they want of their kids, give clear commands, and follow through with a persistence that will not end. The child must comply; there is no alternative. When parents are relentlessly warm, caring, and insistent on compliance, there are few children who will not eventually cave in.

Applying the One-Minute Scolding

We ask parents to stop using their own disciplines for misbehavior. We ask them to use only the One-Minute Scolding until they can apply it anywhere and at any time, consistently and correctly. The Scolding was developed specifically as a bonding exercise, but when we discovered how well it stopped unwanted behaviors, we taught it to all parents who wanted another discipline technique. This technique seems simple and easy to do, but parents are advised that for some, it is very difficult to do correctly and persistently. Parents find it very difficult to abruptly change the expression of feelings from intense anger to intense love and caring. We explain why that is an essential ingredient to the bonding process for these unattached children.

To review briefly how this process works, the first part of the Scolding places the child in a state of arousal. They initially fear the angry parent. When the parent abruptly changes her expression of anger to intense warmth and caring, the child's defenses cannot keep out the warm words because the child's defenses are set up for anger. Before the child can change his defenses to protect himself from the warm, loving words, they flood his psyche and he feels that his parents care for him, that he is a good person, and that his parents will never give up and abandon him and will always try to help him by scolding him whenever he forgets to behave.

Children, and especially teenagers, often find the loving expression of care and concern by the parent difficult to tolerate, and will protest and struggle as though the words were hard and hostile. It is important that the parents insist that the child hear the words of loving care, even through a slammed door.

Parents find themselves uncomfortable doing the One-Minute Scolding. It is difficult not to revert to old punishments and discipline strategies in the heat of battle. They found it relatively easy to do the scolding part, expressing their anger and explaining what rule had been broken. They found it very difficult to be warm and loving while they still felt enraged. They complained bitterly to me when asked to abruptly switch from being angry and upset to acting warm and caring. They felt it the epitome of hypocrisy. It was only when they were convinced there was no other solution to their problem did they reluctantly scold in the prescribed manner. Some redoubled their efforts to find other, less difficult ways to teach their child how to behave. Most families needed six to twelve sessions to effectively turn their child around. If they came back regularly and we had the child and parents fully engaged in the bonding process, and we were satisfied that they would continue the bonding process as taught, we were confident that these parents would form a stable and satisfying attachment to their child.

How Children Resist the One-Minute Scolding

Children sometimes react violently to their loss of control and escalate their misbehaviors. They may become scornful and derisive about their parents' clumsy efforts to institute this new discipline. All children will resist this new parental effort in some way, often in amazingly effective ways. Some children resist violently, running away, acting out aggressively against other individuals or things and escalating the battle for control to a new intensity.

At this point, the role of the therapist is crucial for these "abandoned" children and their parents. The therapist must insist that because the parents love their child, they can use the Scolding consistently and properly. But the therapist also empathizes with their difficulties and their fears. The therapist understands their complaint that it is difficult to make an abrupt change of feeling and to consistently scold every mistake and misbehavior. The therapist rewards the parents' efforts to set reasonable limits and rules. She applauds the parents for expressing intense feeling responses to the child, whether positive or negative, explaining that the child needs these expressions of feelings by the parents. These children have numbed out their feelings, leaving them insensitive to the feelings of others. Parents who express their feelings modestly and tentatively cannot form attachments to these children who were either born insensitive or learned to numb out their feelings.

These numbed-out children feel lonely, empty, and alienated. They tend to respond to intense stimuli that will engage their attention. Sexual feelings of others are very intense, and the numbed-out or insensitive child or adolescent will be drawn to these sexual feelings of others like a moth to a light. Yearning for an attachment, lonely and alienated by their inability to feel the feelings of others, these children and teenagers are unusually vulnerable to being sexually involved with adults. We find this particularly true for pubescent and early adolescent girls. Parents must be unusually sensitive to this possibility and have a plan as to how they would protect their child from inappropriate or dangerous sexual behaviors.

The M & M Game

A third specific technique we encourage parents to use to develop a bond to their unattached child is to use what we call the M & M game. The M & M game is useful for all children who still love candy. The purpose of this game is to compel the child to endure a prolonged, "sweet," infantile experience with her caretaker. The child is seated next to the parent, so that both are comfortable and the child can feel the warmth and closeness of the adult. The parent has ten or twelve M & Ms in her hand and she instructs her child of the rules. The child must close her eyes and stick out her tongue. Mother places the M & M on the child's tongue and tells the child to carefully taste and suck on the candy until she can taste the color of the candy. The youngster may not name the color until the M & M has completely melted in her mouth. The child then guesses the color of the M & M and is congratulated on being correct, whether she is or not. She then gets another M & M and the process is repeated.

While the child is focusing on her mouth and trying to discriminate color by taste, the parent lovingly talks to the child in a low, murmuring voice or she may hum a lullaby-like song. It is important that the parent stroke and touch the child intensely so that the child feels the tenderness and caring of her parent.

When the child "correctly" guesses the color of the candy, the child is rewarded by the enthusiastic approval of the parent. "You are right! You are very good at this game. You get to play again." After ten or twelve M & Ms are eaten, the game ends. When the child protests and wants to continue, the parent empathizes with the desire to continue, but adamantly refuses to play more, and sets the date and time for the next game.

The M & Ms should only be given to the child during this game so that the candy becomes a special candy. The purpose of the game is to get past the child's defenses against the parent's love and warmth, flooding the child with loving words while the child is preoccupied with determining the color of the candy.

The Therapist's Role

The role of the therapist is primarily to assist the parents in their efforts to develop an attachment to their child. Parents frequently become disheartened and discouraged. They feel mistreated and angry with their child. Most dislike the intense feelings of rage and hatred they feel for their child as they experience his feelings of rage and terror. The therapist remains totally convinced that these parents can succeed in engaging their child's feelings and form an attachment. When parents falter and want to give up, thinking that some other parents, school or treatment facility can succeed, the therapist listens empathically, but insists that "things will get better."

The treatment of the unattached child is long and difficult, but failure is disastrous. Parents realize this intuitively and will respond to the therapist's efforts to help them repair the bond. Obviously, the earlier treatment begins the more likely the treatment will be successful, and the treatment process will be much shorter. It is important to emphasize to the parents how painful and difficult the treatment process will be, but it is also important to point out that these children can be successfully treated and a mutually satisfying attachment formed.

Special Case: Foster Children

Any child removed from his own home is in an attachment crisis. One of the primary objectives of a foster home is to minimize the destructive effects of separation from the primary attachment figures. Children can tolerate the temporary loss of an attachment figure much better if there is an available nurturing caretaker present while the child grieves for the absent parent. While the foster parents comfort the grieving child, they are building an attachment to their foster child. The foster parents provide nurture, which includes discipline, control, and comfort to a child who is in intense distress. The child is in a state of high arousal and is actively seeking to be reunited with his parents. He must be encouraged to grieve for his natural parents no matter how badly they treated him. If a child does not grieve (cry, search for, look sad, etc.), the child should be encouraged to do so. If the foster parents recognize the child's distress and respond with understanding and comfort, they will bond to the child and the child to them. This facilitates grieving and minimizes numbing out.

How Separation from Parents Affects a Child

Whenever a young child is separated from his mother and father to whom he is attached, he goes through three predictable stages. He protests vigorously and attempts to recover his mother by crying out for her and physically searching for her. This may last for days or weeks. He then despairs of recovering his mother, but he is still preoccupied and vigilant for her return. This phase usually lasts for several weeks. He then becomes emotionally detached and seems to lose interest in his mother. The emotionally detached period may last for months or years if he does not become attached to another caretaker. A numbed-out child is usually an emotionally detached child.

Both fear behaviors and attachment behaviors serve to protect the child and therefore many of the same conditions elicit both responses. Generally speaking, attachment behavior takes precedence over fear withdrawal if the two are not compatible. The child will often increase his clinging when the attachment figure is also the person who frightens him. The presence or absence of attachment figures or other companions makes an immense difference to the intensity of the child's fear. If the child is uncertain about the availability of the attachment figures, or if the caretaker is unpredictable in protecting or nurturing the child, the child is more likely to respond with fear. This is mistrust.

There are many fear-arousing situations that can happen to a child, but none is likely to be more frightening than the possibility that an attachment figure will be absent or unavailable when needed. When the child is confident that an attachment figure will be available whenever he needs it, he will be less prone to intense or chronic fear. This is basic trust. Children are sensitive to circumstances that affect the building of trust through all the years of immaturity.

It is important to keep in mind that the primary purpose of a caretaker is to lower the child's arousal. Arousal occurs whenever the child is hungry, scared, cold, lonely, or disappointed. Little children are very sensitive and easily aroused or frightened. They are not built to tolerate prolonged, intense arousal. They will always manifest attachment behaviors, such as crying, clinging, whining, or screaming when they are in a state of high arousal. It is the parent's responsibility to lower that arousal by comforting the child.

Mother or Father's presence in an upsetting, fearful situation, like hospitalization, leads to increased trust on the part of the child for adults. There is evidence that shows that the parent/child relationship before and after separation plays a large part in accounting for different outcomes of separation experiences. For example, the child often believes that his misbehaviors just prior to a separation have caused the separation.

Separation has a particularly adverse effect on children whose parents are inclined to be hostile, irritable, or who threaten the child with separation. "If you don't behave, I am going to send you to live in a foster home."

Children suffering from ADHD or attention deficit disorder with hyperactivity are unusually prone to responding to separations and other environmental changes with intense anxiety that often manifests itself as misbehavior. They commonly demonstrate aggressive behavior during separation from their parents and ambivalent behavior (both overly affectionate and angry, aggressive behaviors) after they have returned home after a separation.

The expression of anger during a separation seems to be the child's intuitive efforts to achieve a reunion with the caretaker and possibly discourage further separation. Thus, aggression in the child also has the function of promoting, not disrupting, the attachment process or bonding.

The Permanent Cost of Attachment Failures

If a child cannot or does not turn to his parents for comfort when in distress, this may be termed attachment failure. Loss of the parents or traumatic or prolonged separations usually result in a distortion of, or the abnormal development of, or the failure of the attachment process. The loss of a parent, even when temporary, is a major disruption in the attachment process. The loss of a parent or an attachment figure causes the child to respond in a characteristic way; the child is placed in a state of high arousal for a prolonged period of time, and that causes serious problems for the child. Studies show that prolonged high arousal is associated with high levels of glucocorticoids which may injure or even destroy neurons in the limbic system and cause the child to suffer brain damage, injuring the brain in that area which helps the child to lower his own arousal.

This type of "brain damage" causes the child to be relatively insensitive to the feelings of others. The studies that pertain to this possible explanation of why these children are handicapped emotionally have all been done on nonhuman subjects and therefore we cannot know for sure that similar neurological damage occurs in children. However, the data is solid and it does give us a clinically useful way to understand why these children behave the way they do and even more importantly, it gives us a way to treat them and prevent the disorder.

Minimizing Attachment Crises in Foster Children

Nurturing and attachment-oriented work with children in residential treatment facilities has provided many insights and ideas that can be used by parents and foster parents of unattached, numbed-out children.

If the child must suffer separation from the parents, at or prior to the separation, the child needs clear information about what is to occur. Whenever possible, the child should be presented the information with the assistance of his parent or parents. However, the foster parents and the social worker must be prepared to help the child know what his situation is. It is not helpful to the child to keep important information from him. Information about why, who decided, when, how long, the child's part and other facets about the placement need to be expressed.

You do not have to reveal every detail at the time of separation. Some information should be given at other times. This
includes the answers to such question as: Is it okay for the child
to love the foster parents? Will the parents quit loving the child?
Are the child's feelings acceptable? Can he share them and will he
lose love or care if he does?

Foster parents must define their relationship to their new
child as an alliance for the child's benefit. Their message must be,
"I will take care of you. I want the best for you. When you are not
behaving, I can and will control you." They must teach the child
by direct teaching but more importantly, through example that
feelings are normal, even intensely negative feelings such as fury,
rage, panic, and terror. They must teach the child how to recognize, express, and discharge them for positive and growthful ends.

Their message must be, "It's okay to be sad, mad, and
scared." And then they must show their child an acceptable way to
deal with these intense feelings. It is important that foster parents
be real with their feelings around their child and show him how to
express his feelings appropriately. When the child handles his feelings in an appropriate manner they should reward the expression of
feelings by the child. When the child clearly denies his feelings or
inappropriately expresses them, the foster parents should verbalize
the feelings for him and show him how to express them.

Specifically, the child should learn how to give "I" messages:
"I feel angry, I don't like it when my little brother gets into my
stuff," vs. "You are . . . " Use empathic messages such as, "I am
hearing what you are saying." Then repeat back to the child what
you hear he is telling you. Ask him if you have it right. Help the
child to see that his inappropriate behavior is a "choice that did
not work well for you," and then teach better choices and more
appropriate behavior.

Never fight with a child over issues you cannot control, such as soiling, wetting, and eating. The loss of such battles diminishes your ability to be in control and reinforces the resistant, omnipotent stance of unattached children. Leave the discomfort or the problem with the child and be prepared to help the child with his problem.

Play is healing, both solitary and with peers, siblings, and you, his caretakers. Do not push the child to be so active that he will not be able to engage his fears or feelings, which he may need to do alone in solitary play. Reward the child whenever he engages and expresses his fears. The unattached child does not know how to deal with his feelings appropriately. The parents must teach him how.

Present expectations in nonjudgmental terms, and be clear and accurate with the expression of your feelings about his behaviors. Your feeling will become associated with a behavior. For example, if you respond with horror and intense fear when he runs across a busy street, he will soon learn to become appropriately afraid of that busy street. Conscience can be understood as a multilevel of behaviors, each behavior attached to a specific feeling that was probably learned from the parents.

Discipline and Control in Foster Care

Misbehaviors arise from inappropriate expression of feelings. If the child is not taught differently, the misbehaviors tend to become a habit. Children in treatment facilities have frequently developed a pattern of self-care and should be allowed as much autonomy as possible at first. In addition, they feel they are "being done to" and need a sense of control over their lives. Clear refusal to comply with a wide range of reasonable expectations presented by caregivers is common with such children and must be gently engaged. Obviously, the parents must be in charge and in control.

First of all, the parents must accept, respect, model, push, and support the child in expressing his feelings. When giving an order give a clear explanation of what is wanted, broken down into as small of steps as necessary. Do the task with the child. Use stars, charts, and rewards as a means of having the child measure his own progress. Always accompany rewards with praise and warmth.

When the child resists or defies your orders, keep the conflict focused with the child. He has the problem. He is having trouble obeying a simple order. The parent should firmly insist on compliance in a warm, confident tone of voice. There is no alternative to obeying. The parents does not threaten, "if you don't do it, this will happen!" The parent or caretaker gives orders that will be obeyed even if you have to "wait all day and all night." Time is always on the parent's side. The child will nearly always give in first, but the parents must maintain an attitude that they can wait forever for compliance.

Chapter 15

Holding and Control

In presentations to parents and professionals, several specific techniques have generated a great deal of interest. None has drawn as much interest and controversy as the use of holding and control as a means of renewing, strengthening, and even developing attachments between parent and child. In my clinical experience, unattached children who have numbed out because of prolonged high arousal respond optimally to holding and control techniques and do not seem to respond well to any other therapeutic strategies. Children with a diagnosis of oppositional/defiant disorder also respond well to this technique, often when no other therapeutic approach was effective.

Holding, also known as playing "Who's the Boss?," is only one of the many tools available to those who focus on the attachment process in their work with children and their families. In the absence of the many other attachment steps and tools, holding can be useless and even counterproductive. Therefore, it's important to review the total attachment process (see the discussion in the previous chapter, for example) before exploring the appropriate use of holding and control.

Playing "Who's the Boss?"

In this technique, nurturing control is provided for a child whose coping ability has broken down and is having a tantrum, being destructive, refusing to obey reasonable commands, and being openly defiant. This type of control is done by a caretaker who has been trained to hold or control a child in a loving and nurturing way. It is never necessary to hurt a child and it is nearly always injurious to the attachment process to do so.

A child who is out of control, enraged, or consistently refusing to obey or comply must be protected from hurting himself or others. He needs to be held by warm, loving adults who can control their own anger and fear, and who will see the holding process through to the end. The caretakers will be firm and insist that the child comply with their wishes, and they will hold him or control him until he convinces them that he will obey and behave. They must not stop the holding process until they are sure in their hearts that he will obey and behave immediately after the hold, and for a reasonable time thereafter.

The holding must be protective and nurturing, such as one might give a frightened infant. The primary communication is, "You are out of control, but you won't be hurt, and you will not hurt anyone. I will take care of you until you regain control. I will hold you or control you until you have convinced me that you can obey and behave."

It is essential that once the child has convinced his parents that he will obey and behave, that a period of closeness and warmth is provided by the parents. Both the caretakers and the child will be physically and emotionally drained and exhausted.

The child will be receptive to relating to his caretakers, and the caretakers should be warm, nurturing, touching, tender, and understanding for a considerable period of time after the hold.

However, both the child and the caretaker will likely soon be asleep. The holding should be immediately discussed the next morning in a friendly and open manner. The child will express understandable anger and resentment for the prolonged, stressful period of holding or control. The parent may respond with, "I don't like to do the hold either, but I care for you and I want to be a good parent, so I will play 'Who's the Boss?' whenever you need me to. You are a great kid and I love you very much." The parent constantly teaches the child that a good parent sets limits and controls the child whenever necessary, and does so in a confident, caring manner.

Getting Started

Sometimes you can naturally flow into a hold. However, I encourage most parents to set the stage so that they have the greatest chance for success the first time. Plan a time when both parents are available and willing to take the time to hold the child. Have another adult available to care for the other children, if necessary. Or they can alternate caring for the other children and playing "Who's the Boss?"

Before bedtime is a good time to play "Who's the Boss?" Be prepared to take several hours and tell the child that you are willing to use the whole night, the entire next day and the following evening, if necessary, to help him convince you, the parent, that he will obey and behave. It is probably best to have him in his pajamas, washed and with teeth brushed before you start. Your attitude should be quietly confident. You are totally convinced that he can and will obey and behave. Remember, he has the problem and you are there to help him resolve the problem. More importantly, remember that the child desperately *wants* you to be the boss.

Make yourself comfortable in a big chair. Hold the child in a safe and painless manner. Most small children, those under seven or eight years of age, can be set on the parent's lap with their legs dangling down between the parent's thighs. The child's wrists are held firmly, but gently, so that his arms are comfortably crossed in front of himself. This places the child's back to the parent's chest and the back of the child's head close to the parent's face.

Then tell the child in a warm and confident manner that you are holding him because he has a problem obeying and behaving, and that you will hold him until he has convinced you that he will obey and behave. You assure him that he is a good boy and that he will learn how to obey and behave because you love him and you will help him. He can get up as soon as he has regained control of himself and convinced you that he will obey and behave.

How Children Respond to the "Hold"

Most children will desperately use every weapon and tool in their arsenal to get their parents to stop a "hold." These children are very uncomfortable whenever someone else is in control, and they will try a wide range of strategies to try to get you to stop. Remember that they are very good at taking control, especially if you are unsure about the process. These children often know their parent's weak and vulnerable points. They know which buttons to push and when.

The Tantrum

Children who refuse to obey and are defiant to their parent's wishes often respond to the holding process with outrage and fury. The child will nearly always struggle, tantrum, bellow, and scream—all behaviors that have "worked" in the past to get free and regain control. After all, tantrums are behaviors learned by the child to get his way—so this time he will throw an extreme tantrum.

Be aware that your child will let loose a barrage of profanity. Encourage him to spit them out. "Tell me all those nasty words you have learned. It's okay. I understand how angry and scared you are. You are afraid that if I control you, I will hurt you or leave you. I won't hurt you and I will not let you go until you have convinced me that you are going to obey and behave. I won't hurt you, but I know you are scared." The caretaker provides a running commentary in a low soothing tone that allows the child to see that you are comfortable and confident that he will learn how to obey and behave.

Also, be aware that your child may throw his head back and strike you in the face. This is very painful and unnecessary. Keep your cheek next to his and move your head when he moves his. He may then turn and spit on your face. Just rub the spit off, which always causes great revulsion in the child.

The child will protest that you are hurting him, that you are holding him too tight, and so on. Encourage him to struggle and get away in the following manner: "Show me how strong you are. You think that you have to take care of yourself. You are afraid to trust me, to know what is best for you, to love you and care for you. That's right, struggle hard, don't quit. You are a strong and persistent kid. I like you. I want to be a good Mom (or Dad). Go for it. Don't hold back anything. I know you are a strong kid, but even strong kids get scared and need a mom and a dad when they are scared." You are controlling the child in a warm and caring manner by ordering him to do the very thing that he is doing, struggling to escape your clutches.

You will be using this kind of "double-bind" approach frequently. While the child struggles, you order the child to struggle.

This defines his struggle as an act of obedience to you, which he does not want. If he struggles or tantrums after you have ordered him to do so he is obeying you. You can then praise him for obeying you. If he cusses you tell him that he is being honest in the expression of his feelings. You may add that you prefer that he use straight, honest, "I feel . . . " statements, but if the cussing is the best he can do it is okay with you.

The more important issue is that you do not allow yourself to get angry. If you get angry, it means that you are afraid that you will not be able to persist longer than the child, or that you will not be able to control your temper. If you have a history of being unable to control your anger, *do not do the hold*.

The child's angry behaviors are *always* very upsetting to the parent, and many parents immediately question the wisdom of the "hold." I remind them that we want these children to discharge their terror and rage—which has accumulated over the years when they were abused, abandoned, (psychologically or physically) or neglected. They will perceive the holder as strong enough not to be afraid of this monstrous rage and terror they have been experiencing. They want a strong and caring mom and dad who will not only not abandon them, but also be strong and sensitive enough to comfort them even when they don't want anyone near them.

I encourage these parents to call me for support and encouragement at that time. If my office walls are thick enough so I won't be upsetting my neighbors, I will have the parents do the hold in my office, so that I can be immediately available to help them.

False Agreements

A few very clever children will make subtle efforts to cajole their parents into letting them free—immediately agreeing to anything the parent asks. "See, I'm obeying you. What else do you want?"

Smart children get the message of the "hold" and will capitulate quickly. However, they may not be able to look you in the eye and tell you in a convincing manner that they will obey and behave you. One sign to watch for, if you are unsure, is motor overflow. There is often a small twitch or movement of the eye, head, or body that tells you they have their "fingers crossed." They have no intention of obeying or behaving. Most experienced parents and foster parents are not so easily fooled.

Often, after what seems like a very long struggle, with the child cussing, spitting, scratching, biting, and ordering you to put him down, he may try to bargain with you. "I'll behave. Now let me down!" Watch out for "bossy cooperativeness," which sounds like "Okay, I did what you want, now put me down." This child is still giving orders, which tells you that he still feels he is the boss.

Encourage him, tell him that he is getting close. Tell him to say, "Mama, you are the boss and I will obey you." He will usually refuse or reword the response, which negates the fact that he agrees to obey you.

When children respond with a false positive response, saying they will obey and behave, tell them that they are getting close, but do not relinquish control. In fact, you should begin to quiz them, to see if they are going to obey. They will soon explode in rage when you do not let them free or give them what they want, or if you order them to do something they do not want to do.

A Second Tantrum—and Capitulation

After a period of bargaining, he will usually rage again, more intensely but for a shorter time. Again, encourage him to express his feelings, the best that he can. Ignore the cussing and attacks. If you argue over his words you are accepting his definition of your relationship as at least an equal one. You should continue to insist in a calm and friendly manner that he can convince you that he will obey and behave—and that he is making progress.

After this tantrum, you might get a seductive response; the child may try to sweet-talk you into stopping the "hold" and letting him free. Again, praise him for his efforts and tell him he is making progress, but insist that he tell you again that he will obey and behave in a way that *convinces* you that he sincerely means it.

By this time you will be physically and emotionally exhausted and you will want to believe your child. Beware! He must be totally at peace with his decision that he will now obey and behave and he should be relaxed and relatively happy about his decision. He may still be sobbing and distraught, but he must be convincing to you that he truly means that he trusts you.

The child will eventually begin to relinquish control. He truly wants his parents to be stronger than himself and he wants them to be the boss. Only when he has realized that there is no alternative to "giving up" will he capitulate and agree to obey and behave in a convincing manner to his parents. It is not always easy to tell when this has happened, but typically there is a complete relaxation and a sense of peacefulness in the child. At this point he will usually snuggle up and be "soft" and accept the warm words of comfort and loving gestures from his parents.

The parents will sense that the child has capitulated and is no longer playing games or trying to maintain control. This is an important moment. At that moment the child must be rewarded with praise, hugs, and kisses. His face and hands should be washed with a warm wet cloth, and his pajamas changed, because he will be drenched with sweat. He should be tucked into bed and told that he is a wonderful boy. He will enjoy the warmth and closeness at the end of the hold, but he will be so exhausted at the end he will fall quickly to sleep. Make sure to tell him, "If you get scared or worried in the night, make sure you call for me." The child will sleep like a log and will wake up the next morning relaxed and happy.

Remember that it usually takes about two to four hours of holding or control for most children to relinquish control to their caretakers.

The Parent's Emotions

Most parents find playing "Who's the Boss?" extraordinarily taxing. During the process, their children will experience extremes of terror, rage, and anxiety. The parents, too, will feel totally exhausted and psychologically vulnerable. They will feel like crying because the "hold" was such an intense emotional experience. They will frequently worry that they may be injuring their child by subjecting him to what seems to be a very painful process. They will find the intense feelings of the child and themselves as very unsettling. Often, they find themselves crying in sympathy with the child. Do not worry about these feelings. You are feeling the feelings of the child, and the child has been controlling these feelings for years. By discharging these feelings, the child unburdens himself from them.

If you feel you are getting angry or are not working well with the child, acknowledge this both to yourself and the child. You can use humor, "Wow, you've really got me going." Move away from the issues, have some closeness and stop for a moment. If you get too upset, take a break and wash your face while you let your partner hold your child. It is useful for the parents to encourage and support each other. Holding a child is very difficult for a single parent. They should ask a close friend to be present and be supportive, but the friend or relative should not be asked to do the physical holding. Only the parents or foster parents should do the actual holding.

The Outcome

The result from such a painful and intense interaction between parent and child better be spectacular and it usually is. The next day the child wakes up a different child. He is happy, cheerfully obeys, and behaves like a normal kid. After the initial hold, a child is usually happy, and behaving well for at least a few days. You may well find yourself bruised and vulnerable psychologically while your child seems to have emerged totally unscathed. He is happy that his parents have taken control of the family. But it is difficult to change the patterns of behavior developed over years, so you and your child will regress and start employing old disciplines and behaviors. You must repeat the "hold" when your child needs that kind of help from his parents.

Repeat Holds

Most children require about two or three holds over a period of several weeks. However, many need only one. The child's acceptance of his parent's authority may last for several weeks, but when the parent regresses back to old, maladaptive parenting measures (such as threatening discipline rather than prompt scolding), the child quickly senses that the parents are again reluctant to be the boss. Then the child will again become defiant and disobedient. However, when the parents realize that they have lost control they can repeat the hold. The second or third holds usually do not last long. Some parents find they have to give several holds, but eventually the child becomes compliant and obedient. The appropriate parental attitude is, "I care about you and I will do whatever is necessary to help you. Anytime you tell me or indicate that you need me to hold you so you can behave and obey, I'll do so. I don't care how many times I have to do this. I'll do it because I care about you and love you."

After the initial hold, a child is usually compliant for at least a few days. You will find him surprisingly affable. Many parents dread doing the hold a second time, because the first was such an emotionally draining experience. However, it is most likely that there will be times when the child will again challenge your authority and you will know it is necessary to play "Who's the Boss?" again. Remind yourself that although the "hold" was very stressful for both parent and child, the results were very gratifying, and the next "hold" will not take nearly as long. It will also be easier for both child and parent. When you discuss the possibility of having the child convince you again that you are the boss and he must obey and behave, have the child sit near you. Tell him that he is forgetting that you are the boss and that he is not obeying and he is not behaving. Remind him how good he felt when he felt protected and close to his parents. Many times, this alone will make a difference and holding becomes unnecessary. If the child becomes distant, disobedient, or defiant, you can then tell the child that he is still feeling unsafe and needs more help. You then proceed to hold him again, either right then and there or at a more convenient time for you, the parent. On other occasions, you may tell the child that he is having a problem remembering who the boss is in the family and that you will help him. You can tell him that you will play "Who's the Boss?" later, and then set a time when it is convenient.

Older Children and Teenagers

Older children and teenagers cannot be held. They can be contained in a room, together with the parents, and the entire holding technique used without physically holding the child. It is often just as effective, but may take longer.

The child is told that he, Mom, and Dad are going to work out this problem about behaving and obeying until the child convinces the parents that he understands what the parents want, and fully intends to comply with their wishes. The child will usually refuse and often try to leave the room. The parents should firmly, but lovingly, insist that the child remain in the room until the process is completed, and express confidence that the child can do it. The parents should passively block the door and not allow the child to leave. Often, he will escape and run from the house. This should be anticipated and the child told, "This is not a prison. We do not have bars on the doors or windows. If you leave, we will look for you, bring you home, and then we will just scold you for a minute and then resume playing 'Who's the Boss?' Don't worry, we love you and we care about you. We want the best for you and we will do everything we can for you. Now you must convince us that you know that we must be the boss, and that you will obey us and behave. You are a good boy and we know you can do it."

The older child will often go on a rampage and try to destroy things. Again, you may have to physically restrain him from hurting you or destroying things, but you must make every effort not to hurt the child. You must tell him that you are not going to hurt him, but he must obey because that is what is best for him. The parents' voices must be confident, soothing, calm, and tender. The parents can list all the reasons why the child will be in distress. Parents can empathize and verbalize their under-standing of the pain, anger, and rage felt by the child because of past painful events. The parents assure the child that they want what is best for him and that they know it is best for him that he behaves and obeys this parents.

More often than not, the adolescent out of control is unable to tolerate the warmth and the insistence for obedience and good behavior. He or she will usually run the first time. Tell the teenager that you understand and that you will keep trying until the young-ster eventually listens and hears the warmth and caring in you voice and your behavior. The child desperately wants to behave and obey, but the rage and the fear are too intense. Tell him that you will look for him if he runs away, and that you will leave the door open so that he can return when he feels better. Tell him to take a jacket if it is cold, and not to stay out too late. He must be left with the option of returning to a warm and caring home.

The numbed-out adolescent has great difficulty dealing with parental warmth and tenderness. The parents should respect the teenager's need for more distance until he adjusts to the new feeling environment. Above all, the parent must remember that even large, muscular teenagers often feel like helpless, vulnerable little children and need comforting. They may not allow you to put them on your lap, but they will usually allow you to comfort them with your voice. As their fear diminishes, their anger often pours forth in angry, nasty words. Strong parents allow those words to pass without attention to the content, "You are a bitch," etc., and instead engage the feelings by verbalizing them for the teenager. "You are mad at me for not allowing you to go to that party. You want me to trust you not to drink or take drugs when everyone else is doing it. I understand, but I have to be a good parent, and a good parent would never put his kid in a difficult situation like that. You can't go, but it is okay to rant and rave at me. Get it out of your system so it doesn't eat at you and get you into trouble. Don't worry about me. Four-letter words have never hurt me. I don't like them, but if you have to use them to express your anger, go right ahead."

Strong parents encourage the discharge of feelings by their children, knowing that children will have difficulty expressing them appropriately without practice. When parents encourage the expression of feelings, the child learns how to behave while feeling strong feelings. If the parent listens to the discharge of rage and hatred with understanding and caring, the child learns that these feelings do not have to result in abnormal behavior.

Checklists

The following issues should be carefully assessed prior to the use of holding.

Indications That Holding Is an Appropriate Approach

1. *Is a Full Range of Care Available?* Our first criterion must be that the full range of care to support the attachment process is being provided. A caretaker must be available and willing to sensitively and appropriately respond to the child, particularly lowering the child's arousal whenever necessary. With such care, the child will improve in all developmental areas. If, after a reasonable time, progress is not noted, then holding is appropriate.

2. *Does the Child Avoid Closeness?* The child continues to not allow closeness (e.g., avoiding caregiver nurturing and interactions, flinching or jumping away from being touched).

3. *Does the Child Resist Obedience?* There is wide-ranging and persistent resistance to complying with expectations of caregivers (i.e., not trusting control of others).

4. *Does the Child Exhibit Symptoms of Unattachment?* The child presents symptoms of a lack of attachment, such as poor eye contact, lack of conscience development, and behaviors aimed at preventing closeness, such as withdrawal, aggressive behavior, promiscuous behavior, and overcompetence.

(Please note that one symptom of attachment disruption has been excluded from these criteria—psychotic behavior. Such a symptom requires referral for psychiatric services, and holding is not appropriate for such children within a foster home setting or with the natural parents.)

5. *Is the Child Anxious or Fearful?* The child is unable to deal with important life issues because of extreme anxiety and fearful-

ness (i.e., the child requires a maximum sense of safety and security in order to address the issues).

Issues That Affect Whether Holding Can Be Used

1. *Age and Size.* Children entering adolescence and teenagers should not be held. Children whose size and strength preclude easy control should not be physically held. These children should be controlled verbally.

2. *Available Time.* Holding is a process that must be followed through to completion. One cannot accurately predict how much time is required; therefore, you must have an open-ended schedule that allows as much time as necessary. We have found that evening is the best time and you should be prepared to spend up to four hours for the first hold.

3. *Preparing Others to Help.* Holding a child should be approached in a relaxed and supportive manner. Therefore, anyone who is participating should know what they are getting into. This is particularly true if you have another adult in the house to help. They must be thoroughly briefed on the theory and the procedure, and if they are unable to wholeheartedly support you, postpone the hold or have the person leave.

4. *Choice of Place.* The child often releases pent-up fear, sadness, terror, and rage, and does so noisily and often with profanity. Others not involved, like neighbors and grandparents, can interfere or misunderstand what is occurring. The best place to play "Who's the Boss?" is in the child's bedroom or in the parent's bedroom, if necessary. If your neighbors are within hearing distance, warn them that they may hear a lot of noise.

5. *Availability of Attachments.* Remember, attachments are a "two-way street." A true attachment is both a bond of child to adult and adult to child. If there are two parents, both of them

should be present during the hold and be willing to be warm, caring, and tender, as well as strong as steel. A child is NEVER harmed by forming attachments to caring adults, provided the adult separates from the child in an appropriate and thoughtful way. Foster parents may have a child for only a few weeks, and because of their willingness to attach to the child, they often provide an attachment-memory that will provide hope and faith in the possibility of a successful attachment in the future.

6. *Granting Permission to Feel.* One result of holding is an increased awareness and ability to accurately express feelings. Will those parenting the child allow and support feeling expression? If not, you may be setting the child up for future problems.

Self-Assessment for the Potential Caretaker

1. *Knowing the Child.* Do you know what the pertinent issues are for this child? Do you know his fears and sensitivities? Do you know how he was abused, neglected, or abandoned?

2. *Handling Strong Emotions.* Can you handle your own anger and maintain a genuine, warm, caring, and confident attitude while you are holding an enraged, strong, persistent kid who is also terrified? Are you willing to be cussed out, hit, bit, spit upon, and accused of being a terrible person while you are holding the child? Are you willing to spend hours the first time so that you do not have to repeat the holding more than a few times?

3. *Familiarity with the Attachment Process.* Do you understand the attachment process? Are you willing to abide by the rules and maintain a quiet, warm, and confident attitude while you are doing the hold?

4. *Ability to Express Your Feelings.* Are you comfortable in expressing your feelings and willing to hear and reward the expression of feelings by your children?

5. *Understanding the Process*. Do you understand what is involved in holding, and see it as supportive, rather than as "whipping the child into shape"?

6. *Openness to Attachment*. Do you have an appropriate desire and openness to being attached to the child and the child attached to you?

Cautions d Complementary Approaches

In California, the social workers in the Department of Social Services forbid their foster parents to hold their charges because they define the hold as a form of child abuse. However, parents who use the technique as described in this book have never been charged with child abuse. A basic underlying tenet of this parenting technique is that the child is never to be hurt, physically or emotionally. Adoptive parents and birth parents all over the country have used the hold, nearly always with good results. I have used it in my own practice wherever indicated for over thirty years and have found that it works where no other form of treatment works. It is important to remember that the child wants the parents to be strong and in control; he wants his parents to be stronger than himself. This is why the child invariably responds after the "hold" with calm acceptance, demonstration of honest affection, and natural obedience to his parent's requests.

Holding, however, is not a panacea. The child must also experience other bonding interactions with his parents. These include appropriate caretaking responses to any situation that places the child in a state of high arousal. The parent's response should always strive to comfort the child and lower his arousal. The parent plays hide-and-seek and other bonding games. The M & M game can be useful as a weekly bonding process. The child is disciplined using the One-Minute Scolding, because this bonding technique is particularly useful for children who have become numbed out because of prolonged high arousal. Caretakers must use many other attachment-oriented parenting techniques or the hold will not help the child develop a trusting relationship to his caretakers and therefore obey and behave.

The child and parent should be encouraged to practice being close or intimate at other times, and not just when disciplined. Closeness must not only be sought when there is a problem. The purpose of attachment is closeness or intimacy, not holding or being in control. If the parent and the child are close or intimate, the parent knows when and why the child is upset and in a state of high arousal, and what to do about the problem. The child will trust the parent when the parent can consistently and effectively lower his arousal. If the parent can comfort the child immediately, the bond becomes much stronger.

Bibliography

Babcock, Dorothy, and Terry Keepers. *Raising Kids OK.* New York: Grove Press, 1976.

Bach, George, and Herb Goldberg. *Creative Aggression: The Art of Assertive Living.* New York: Avon, 1975.

Biller, Henry, and Dennis Meredith. *Father Power.* New York: David McKay, 1974.

Bowlby, John. *Maternal Care and Mental Health.* Geneva: World Health Organization, 1951.

_____. *Child Care and the Growth of Love.* Harmondsworth, England: Penguin, 1965.

_____. *Attachment and Loss,* Vols. I, II, III. New York: Basic Books 1973–1980.

_____. "The Making and Breaking of Affectional Bonds: Aetiology and Psychopathology in Light of Attachment Theory," *British Journal of Psychiatry* 130 (1977): 201–210.

Branden, Nathaniel. *The Psychology of Self-Esteem.* New York: Bantam, 1971.

_____. *Breaking Away.* New York: Bantam, 1972.

Brazelton, T. B., et al. *Parent-Infant Interaction,* Ciba Foundation Symposium 33. New York: Elsevier, 1975.

Briggs, Dorothy Corkille. *Your Child's Self-Esteem.* Garden City: Doubleday, 1975.

Coopersmith, Stanley. *The Antecedents of Self-Esteem.* San Francisco: W. H. Freeman, 1967.

Dobson, James. *Dare to Discipline.* New York: Bantam, 1970.

_____. *Emotions: Can You Trust Them?* Glendale, CA: Regal, 1980.

Dobson, Fitzhugh. *How to Parent.* Los Angeles: Nash, 1970.

_____. *How to Discipline with Love.* New York: Rawson Associates, 1977.

Dunn, Judy. *Distress and Comfort.* Fontana: Open Books, 1977.

Eisenberg, L. "The Fathers of Autistic Children," *American Journal of Orthopsychiatry* 27 (1957): 715–725.

Eriksen, Erik. *Childhood and Society.* New York: W. W. Norton, 1950.

_____. "Identity and the Life Cycle," *Psychological Issues* (monograph) Vol. I, No. 1: 68.

Farmer, Bill. "No Paddle Ball in Sweden," *Parade,* March 16, 1980.

Freud, Anna. *Beyond the Best Interests of the Child.* New York: The Free Press, Macmillan, 1973.

Freud, Anna and Dorothy Burlingham. *Infants Without Families.* New York: International Universities Press, 1973.

Friedman, Robert, et. al. "Parent Power: A Holding Technique in the Treatment of Omnipotent Children," *International Journal of Family Counseling,* 68073.

Ginnot, Hiam. *Between Parent and Child.* New York: Macmillan, 1965.

Glueck, E. T., and Sheldon Glueck. "Identification of Potential Delinquents at Two to Three Years of Age," *International Journal of Social Psychiatry* (1966).

Greenberg, Martin, and Normal Morris. "Engrossment: The Newborn's Impact Upon the Father," *American Journal of Orthopsychiatry* 44, no. 4 (1974).

Howell, Mary C. "Employed Mothers and Their Families," *Pediatrics* 52, no. 3 (1973): 14.

James, Muriel. *What Do We Do With Them Now That We've Got Them?* Reading, Mass.: Addison-Wesley, 1974.

James, Muriel, and Dorothy Jongeward. *Born to Win: Transactional Analysis with Gestalt Experiments.* New York: Signet, 1978.

Johnson, Thomas. "Guidelines for Discipline," published by the Youth Service Bureau and the San Diego County Probation Department, 1979.

Kempe, Ruth S., and C. Henry Kempe. *Child Abuse*. Fontana: Open Books, 1977.

Klaus, Marshall H., and John H. Kennell. *Maternal-Infant Bonding*. St. Louis: C.V. Mosby, 1976.

Kohlberg, L. *Stages in the Development of Moral Thought and Action*. New York: Holt, Rinehart, and Winston, 1969.

Kotelchuck, Milton. "The Nature of the Child's Ties to His Father," Ph.D. dissertation, Harvard University, Boston, April 1972. p. 37–44.

_____, et al. "Infantile Reaction to Parental Separation When Left Alone with Familiar and Unfamiliar Adults," *Journal of Genetic Psychology* 126 (1975).

_____, et al. "Separation Protest in Infants in Home and Laboratory," *Developmental Psychology* 11 (1975).

_____, et al. "Father Interaction and Separation Protest," *Developmental Psychology* 9 (1973): p. 50–60.

Lamb, Michael. "Proximity Seeking Attachment Behaviors: A Critical Review of the Literature," *Genetic Psychology Monographs* 6 (1976): p. 12–18.

Levine, James A. *Who Will Raise the Children: New Options for Fathers (and Mothers)*. New York: J. B. Lippincott, 1976.

Lowen, Alexander. *The Language of the Body*. New York: Macmillan, 1971.

_____. *Bioenergetics*. New York: Penguin, 1976.

Maslow, Abraham. *Towards a Psychology of Being*. New York: D. Van Nostrand, 1962.

Mitchell, Gary, William Redican, and Jody Gomber. "Lessons from a Primate: Males Can Raise Babies," *Psychology Today,* April 1974.

Parker, Ross, and Sandra O'Leary. "Father-Mother-Infant Interaction in the Newborn: Some Findings, Some Observations, and Some Unresolved Issues," in K. Riegel and J. Meachem, eds., *The Developing Individual in a Changing World,* Vol. 11. The Hague: Norton, 1975.

Redican, William, and Gary Mitchell. "Play Between Adult Male and Infant Rhesus Monkeys," *American Zoology* 14 (1974): p. 78.

Restak, Richard. "The Origins of Violence," *Saturday Review,* May 12, 1979.

_____. *The Brain: The Last Frontier.* New York: Doubleday, 1979.

Rogers, Carl. *On Becoming a Person.* Boston: Houghton Mifflin, 1961.

Rutter, Michael. *Maternal Deprivation Reassessed.* Middlesex, England: Penguin, 1972.

Salk, Lee. *What Every Child Would Like His Parents to Know.* New York: David McKay, 1975.

Satir, Virginia. *Peoplemaking.* Palo Alto: Science and Behavior Books, 1972.

"Saving the Family," *Newsweek,* Special Report, May 15, 1978.

Schaffer, Rudolph. *Mothering.* Fontana: Open Books, 1977.

Scharlatt, Elizabeth, et al. *Kids: Day In and Day Out.* New York: Simon and Schuster, 1979.

Schutz, Will. *Profound Simplicity.* New York: Bantam, 1980.

Seay, B., B. K. Alexander, and H.F. Harlow. "Maternal Behavior of Socially Deprived Rhesus Monkeys," *Journal of Abnormal and Social Psychology* 69, no. 4 (1964): 347.

Silberman, Melvin, and Susan Wheelan. *How to Discipline Without Feeling Guilty.* New York: Hawthorn, 1980.

Toffler, Alvin. *Future Shock.* New York: Random, 1970.

Van Buren, Abigail. "Dear Abby," *The San Diego Union,* May 2, 1979.

Viscott, David. *How to Live with Another Person.* New York: Arbor House, 1974.

Index

ALSO AVAILABLE FROM ADAMS MEDIA:

The Everything Games Book

*T*he Everything Games Book has everything you'll need for hours of family entertainment. Not only will you find new and exciting games to play, but you'll have a complete source of easy-to-follow rules and regulations for hundreds of activities. Whether you are planning a party or just spending a rainy afternoon at home, *The Everything Games Book* provides challenging fun and friendly competition for all ages and every level of play.

Trade paperback, $12.95
ISBN: 1-55850-643-8

Available wherever books are sold.

**For more information, or to order, call 800-872-5627
or visit www.adamsmedia.com**

Adams Media Corporation, 260 Center Street, Holbrook, MA 02343

ALSO AVAILABLE FROM ADAMS MEDIA:

The Everything Bedtime Story Book

T*he Everything Bedtime Story Book* is a wonderfully original collection of 100 stories that will entertain the entire family. You can change bedtime from a dreaded task to a wonderful family experience, as you share some of literature's great children's classics. Perfect for any age—from babies to toddlers, and beyond—*The Everything Bedtime Story Book* will inspire young readers, and take parents back on a trip to their own childhood.

Trade paperback, $12.95
ISBN: 1-58062-147-3

Available wherever books are sold.

**For more information, or to order, call 800-872-5627
or visit www.adamsmedia.com**

Adams Media Corporation, 260 Center Street, Holbrook, MA 02343